The Schoolhouse

A Hickory Grove Novel

THE SCHOOLHOUSE

Published by:

Elizabeth Bromke

White Mountains, Arizona

Prologue: 1988

Becky tugged open the rusty metal drawer and reached inside, pawing blindly around.

"I can't *believe* there's no bookshelf in this place. No corner library or something," she muttered as she withdrew her hand to find it laced over with cobwebs.

The girls played at the schoolhouse nearly every weekend and some weekdays, too. Until now, they hadn't done much digging around. But when they uncovered a secret drawerful of chalk, it occurred to them that other treasures might be lurking in the nooks and crannies of Hickory Grove's own one-room schoolhouse. To the town, the schoolhouse was little more than an abandoned building. To the girls, it was an enchanted palace. The perfect play house.

"Maybe they didn't have libraries back then," Maggie replied, shrugging and snapping her gum.

Becky snorted, pushed up on her tippy toes, and stuck her hand deeper into the creaking cavern. "Of course they did. Libraries are ancient. And even the Dewey Decimal system was invented in the 1800s."

"What's that?"

Becky froze, her hand alighting on the obvious sensation of dust-covered paperbacks. "*Yes*," she hissed, then turned to her friend, her tone dropping into disgust. "You're joking. *Everyone* knows the Dewey Decimal system." Disdain splashed across the ten-year-old's face.

How could she be best friends with someone this careless? This *indifferent*? Last week's vocabulary words clung to her brain. *Indifferent*: (adjective) *uncaring about; lacking interest.*

She glared hard at Maggie.

The freckly redhead rolled her eyes. "I was absent that day," Maggie replied meekly as she trudged across the room and slumped into a wooden desk. Dust swirled behind her in the afternoon sun that poured in from the west windows.

Even the dust is annoyed with her, Becky thought. She knew better than to trust this false pouting.

Being both the more serious girl and the older one, Becky pulled her newly discovered books from the drawer then slammed the metal filing cabinet shut, victory and accomplishment swelling inside her. "Okay, well, I'll explain it later. Just play along, all right?"

A sigh filled Maggie's little body. Becky gave her a sharp look.

"Yes, Miss Linden," Maggie replied, licking her lips and rising to follow the blonde girl over a sunken wooden floor and to the old teacher's desk that half-stood, half-leaned in the corner.

Like the floor that was swallowing it, the desk was made of thick wood. Cedar, probably. Becky had already asked Grandbern about it, but he didn't remember. She was desperate to know if that desk was the same one that Grandbern's Aunt Edna had sat at when he was a student and she was his teacher back in the 1940s.

Carefully scooting the chair out and perching herself on the edge (dry rot had overcome the wicker center), Becky set the books in a neat pile in front of her.

"Here, Maggie," she said, pushing the pile closer to the far side of the desk. "Pretend you found these on the *shelves*."

Maggie nodded, picked them up and set them back down with a flourish. "I'd like to check these out, ma'am," she trilled.

Becky reached for the stapler she'd brought from home and used it to "scan" the back of each book. As she passed the first one to Maggie, its title slipped through her lips in a sing-song voice. She forced herself to hide her glee at unearthing the antique collection in order to preserve the authenticity of their game.

"*The Wizard of Oz.* You'll enjoy this one, young lady. It's a classic, you know." Becky dropped her chin and studied Maggie over the top of the wire-framed glasses she'd found in Memaw's roll-top desk.

Maggie continued her role without a hitch. "Why yes, Miss Linden. It's one of my favorite books in the whole world."

Becky eyed her knowingly but was glad to be back in character. "It's an excellent selection, dear." She flipped to the next. "Ah, what do we have here? *Easy Steps in Reading*? Hmm." Becky tried for condescension but Maggie would have no part.

"Indeed, Miss Linden. I'm practicing my letters."

Becky moved on to the next. An illustrated cover glowed through the caked-on dust, and she immediately forgot they were playing. "Oh my gosh, Mag! Look!" She pulled the delicate glasses from her nose and set them on the desk, turning the book over in her hands. "*Little House in the Big Woods*!"

Maggie leaned over the desk and tried to make out the words upside down. "I can't read it."

"Maggie, it's *Little House on the Prairie*! The first one!" Becky slowly lifted the front cover as if it might disintegrate in her fingers.

Just then, a hollering voice blew in from beyond the gaping front door. The girls squinted up, and Becky realized the sun had sunk lower into the trees outside.

The voice became clearer, though she already knew who it was. "Girls! You all get-on-out of there, now. You hear me?"

Maggie didn't move. Becky drew the cover closed and held the book against her chest, leaving behind the others for another day. Another game.

She then stood and ran to the door. "We're comin', Grandbern!" He was just down the lane, a crooked figure looming at the edge of what used to be some sort of driveway up to the schoolhouse. He had a handkerchief in his hand, and he was using it to dab his forehead just below a neat comb-over.

Becky looked back at Maggie, who'd begun thumbing the other books as though they held half as much value as *Little House*. "You comin'?" she called back.

"Yeah, okay." Maggie blew out a sigh, pushed the other two books against the wall, and dragged herself to the door where she waved limply at Grandbern.

Becky pointed at the two bikes that leaned against the white wood siding. "We'll ride home, okay?" She and Maggie exchanged their goodbyes and each took off toward her own house—Maggie would return to a trailer with her aunt; Becky would return to her grandparents' farm.

Grandbern tucked the red handkerchief neatly into his breast pocket and ambled back down the dusty lane toward his truck, muttering as he went.

Becky never could put a number on his age. He might be fifty or eighty. All she really knew was that he had worked his whole life and was still working. Hard. That and what her mama had told her. Grandbern was faster than a fox. To this day he could outrun Becky or even her brother, Ben, who was the fastest boy at Hickory Grove Elementary School.

It was mid-July in Hickory Grove which meant no school. Becky and Ben's mom worked around the clock at Mally's Diner. If the kids were out of school, Grandbern and Memaw watched them, giving Becky and Ben more freedom than Patsy Linden would have. But a working mom had little choice in the matter.

Sometimes, like when Grandbern had something important to do with the farm or if he and Memaw had a doctor's appointment, Becky and Ben would have to hang out in the break room at the diner.

The farm wasn't far, but Grandbern was a slow driver and wouldn't get back nearly as fast as Becky. During her ride, she chided herself for never having found the book before. They'd been playing in the abandoned schoolhouse for over a year now. She'd read every piece of graffiti—new and old—and tried out every creaky, old desk.

Of all the curios there, the metal filing cabinet never struck her interest when she and Maggie stumbled inside one sunny spring morning. Metal filing cabinets didn't seem as interesting as the little wood stove that anchored the room. Or the old-fashioned bell that sat in a circle of rotted wood.

They often played "House" or "Library " in the schoolroom, and Becky and Maggie would bring their own toys and books, careful to leave with them every day just in case a vagabond came across the place and wanted to steal their goods. They chose to be circumspect with their movements inside the house. One false step could pop them right down into the earth. So a full-blown inspection was not an immediate priority.

Of course, as the months wore on, the girls grew more comfortable, making a little home amid the daddy long-legs and mossy window sills.

Finding those books meant nothing to Maggie. After all, Maggie was already interested in boys, and boys meant nothing to Becky.

But the *books* meant everything to Becky. It was a living history. Right there in the schoolhouse. Proof of generations past. Kids from yesteryear. Kids who went to school and read stories just like she did. Maybe those kids even treasured their books. Maybe they didn't want to leave them behind.

She careened up the dirt road to the house, dust billowing in her wake as she laid on her brakes and propped the bike against the porch, running inside to check for fresh-brewed sweet tea.

The kitchen and living room were empty. No Ben. No Memaw. Alone and sweet tea-less, she sank into the front sitting chair and pulled her book bag onto her lap, excited to thoroughly examine her newest treasure.

"Rebecca Marie." Grandbern's voice interrupted her for the second time that evening, and she was getting irritated.

She pulled the flap shut and tapped her foot on the floor, staring at him expectantly. "Yessir?"

"Get your things together, young lady. I'm driving you to the diner tonight, 'cause Memaw and I are heading into New Albany."

"What? Where's Ben? Does he have to go?"

"He's already there."

"Why are you going to New Albany?" This was news to her. Grandbern and Memaw never went anywhere, especially at nighttime. Why were they headed off at *nighttime*? She braced herself for a scandal.

Her granddad grinned from ear to ear and pulled his handkerchief out, dabbing at his temples once more before folding it back up and tucking it into that little pocket on his plaid button-down shirt. He adjusted his suspenders nervously, avoiding Becky's even gaze. At last, he let out a little laugh and looked past his granddaughter to the master bedroom.

Becky whipped her head around, wincing as her braids cut across her face. Stepping from the doorway was Memaw Linden, dressed to the nines in what Becky could only describe as a disco ball. Memaw locked eyes with Grandbern and Becky felt a gag form in her throat. "Aw, come on, you all," she whined from the sitting chair.

"I'm taking Memaw on an overnight date to the big city, Rebecca," he answered, his eyes lingering on his wife. Memaw smiled beneath her hairdo—swooping white waves that weren't about to go anywhere. No matter how much dancing she and Grandbern planned to do.

"Ew," Becky whispered to herself, careful to avoid a scolding. Then, she raised her voice in an earnest question for the two of them. "Why are you dressed up?"

Her discomfort turned to curiosity. She'd grown up with Memaw and Grandbern occasionally holding hands or offering each other a dry peck on the cheek. Nothing unreasonable for a married couple of a certain age. And Memaw *did* have a stack of romance novels teetering so high on her bedside table that Becky figured she was going for a world record.

But not having ever met her own father and with Maggie's parents out of the picture...well, *real* romance was completely unfamiliar to the ten-year-old.

"We're celebrating our thirtieth wedding anniversary, darlin'," Memaw answered as she smoothed the unsmoothable fabric of her dress. "Let's get goin', you two. Jump in the back of the truck, Rebecca."

Becky did as she was told.

The ride to the diner was bumpy, and she clutched her satchel for dear life, worried each rock in the road would send the book catapulting out of her bag and under a tire to be squashed like a bug.

Thankfully, that didn't happen, and she hopped out at the diner with her satchel and treasure intact. She waved her grandparents off and trudged around to the back of the diner.

There, making figure eights in the back lot, was Becky's twin brother, Ben.

"Hey, Ben!" she called out to him. He offered a stoic nod before attempting a tricky maneuver on his back tire. Worried she'd distract him and cause a fall, Becky scuttled into the back door, down a short hall, and to the break room.

Dinner smells instantly clung to her overalls, and Becky's irritation returned. She didn't mind spending time anywhere so long as she had a book, but she hated going home each night smelling like greasy burgers, especially when they never had enough hot water to go 'round for a proper nightly shower.

Becky knew her mom would sense her presence at any moment so she didn't waste time in pulling the book from her bag and flipping the cover back open to take a closer look at what her school librarian had taught her was the copyright page. She had scoffed at the woman. Who cared about any of the dates the book was printed? Who cared if it was printed ten times? All a reader really needed to know was who wrote the book so she could get her hands on more books if she liked the author.

But this book had only one year: 1932.

"Hm," Becky mumbled, flipping the page cautiously to the dedication and then Chapter One. Becky had already read *The Little House in the Big Woods*, of course. But that didn't mean she wasn't about to read it again right here, right now. Still, she needed a moment. She wanted to take it all in.

Flipping back to the copyright stuff again, she noticed she'd missed the title page. Her finger slid down along the sharp edge, nearly causing a paper cut. As the delicate paper settled against her right thumb, she saw, for the first time, a list of names scrawled on the inside of the cover, as though it were a school textbook, passed on from class to class.

Intrigued, she pressed a finger to each name in the list. Some names were written in all capitals. Some in childish scribble. Some looked like nicknames. Some full names. Each one was added to the book in a different pen or even a pencil and only two included a year. It was a hapless list, to be sure. Such reckless record-keeping was a pet peeve of Becky's. She was a list-maker. A note taker. A diary-writer. A calendar-keeper.

Now, as Becky sank into the tired floral cushions of the break room couch, she went back up and down the list, looking for any Lindens or even a familiar first name. She knew full well that nearly all of her own family had attended the one-room schoolhouse back in the olden days.

There were no Lindens.

But the first name was Eddie, and she was pretty sure she had a third cousin named Eddie. Twice removed. Ancient. She met him at a reunion one time.

As for the rest of the students, well they were nearly all familiar. Hickory Grove was a small town. Everybody knew everybody. And Becky was pretty sure she knew the families of the kids who'd read this here book.

After Eddie was Norma Reynolds. *Of the Reynolds bunch, no doubt.*

Then Patrick Thomas Flanagan. *Probably Jake's pa-paw.*

Rita Gale. Mrs. Gale's . . . mom?

Bobby Daley. Yep. The Daleys.

June Zick. The Zicks were the nicest family in town.

Margaret Ann Hart. Same last name as that guy who asked Mama out on a date.

Jody Kay. She knew the Kays!

Sarah "Sally" Engel. *Sounded familiar.*

And, finally, Darla Durbin.

Darla was the standout. Becky didn't know any Durbins. None at all.

Chapter 1

Becky lowered the volume on her radio and grabbed the plastic walkie-talkie from her cup holder. "Tango Hotel Echo Oscar. Come in. Over." She'd learned the code words for Theo's name just before they left.

"Mom, it's not funny anymore," his boyish voice crackled in reply. She looked hard through her windshield to see if he was glancing back in his rearview or side mirror, but his car was too crammed for her to even spot his head.

Another mom would find the driving arrangements unsafe. But they were fine. A moving truck would have cost money— money neither Becky nor her eighteen-year-old son had as they packed up their whole lives into a two-seater sedan and a little yellow truck.

Anyway, this was an adventure. A cross-country adventure. Arizona to Indiana. Sight-seeing during pit stops. A few overnighters.

Since they had all summer to prep for the move, Becky forced Theo to leave a couple days earlier than they had to. He couldn't get into his dorm until late August. The drive would take them about three days if they stayed the course. She wanted to see a little bit of the countryside together. Like a vacation.

Theo was a good kid. He obliged her on stopping in Abilene, Texas. He didn't even whine when all they did was stand at a gas station and stare around. But he had asked for clarification.

"Why are we stopping here, again?"

"It's my favorite song," she'd answered, breathing in the smell of dust and petroleum.

Of course, he did point out that she said that about nearly any song she recognized. His theory was only proven when they also stopped in Amarillo, Texas, for burritos.

Theo was dutifully sorrowful as they solemnly strode from their hot vehicles and up to the memorial for the Oklahoma City Bombing.

And Theo didn't even complain when they got lost in the Mark Twain National Forest. It was far off course, but Becky figured it was worthy of admiration. Theo pretended to agree.

There wasn't much to the forest, but Becky could at least tell people she had been there. Grandbern wouldn't be very interested. Neither would Memaw. Maggie would appreciate it on behalf of Becky, though.

Maggie.

Becky was anxious for the reunion with her best friend. They hadn't seen each other since she left Indiana for Tucson eighteen years before. A lot could happen in eighteen years. A lot *did* happen. At first, she and Maggie stayed close via late-night phone calls and even handwritten letters. The calls became fewer over the years. Letter writing vanished entirely. Once emails and social media took the world by storm, they were too far gone for any meaningful conversations, opting instead to simply *like* and *react* and *comment* on the news that each one decided to put online for the world to see.

But it was harder to catch up with someone who you kept tabs on all the time. If it weren't for the Internet, Becky wouldn't know that Maggie had three kids and three caesarians. Maggie could tell her so in person. It would come as a happy shock. A good story. Instead, Becky would have to sit there, across from Maggie, pretending she didn't already have a good sense of Maggie's life.

Keeping in touch online didn't really feed their friendship; it hamstrung it. Or, at least, that's how Becky worried things would go. Stilted conversations about how each one of them had already seen this or already knew that.

Becky sighed and followed Theo down a beautiful narrow lane to his dormitory. They parked outside an immaculate older building.

It reminded her of when she first moved into her own dorm room at The University of Arizona. She swallowed hard and dabbed at her eyes with the pads of her fingers in time for Theo to jump out of his Civic and jog back to her. She began to unbuckle her seatbelt but he waved a hand, effectively stopping her in action. Confused, she opened the door. He stood near it, still. Awkward. Excited.

Her beautiful only child. The boy who mended her heart over the course of nearly two decades. The boy who kept her in Arizona despite her deep need to run home. The boy who turned her from a girl into a mother.

He smiled apologetically and let her know that they'd be saying their goodbyes here. His new roommates just texted and the whole floor was about to grab pizza. *He'd* pull his stuff from her truck real quick. *He'd* haul it up. *He'd* unpack. Later.

Without her.

***

Five hugs and twice as many kisses on the cheek weren't enough. Becky wanted to explore campus. She wanted to help Theo decide which side of the room would be his. She wanted to remind him not to put up any posters of half-naked girls or silly beer pong scenes. She wanted to make his bed for him one last time before standing in the doorway where she would feel a sense of closure.

Maybe she'd grab herself a cup of coffee on the quad or wherever the Fighting Irish got their coffee while on campus.

Briefly, Becky thought of renting a motel room and meeting back up with Theo later that day or maybe tomorrow. Or maybe she could hole up in a restaurant off-campus. She pulled her phone and started to call him but then switched to a text. Scratching her head, she wasn't quite sure what to say. What was best.

So she let it be.

Anyway, they were close enough. She'd be down the road four hours or so.

Next weekend. She'd drive back up next weekend. After he was settled. Becky knew these initial social opportunities were crucial. They would define his entire college career. Maybe his whole life. Much like her initial social opportunities defined hers.

***

With a hollow heart and empty stomach, she left the school, opting for a drive-through dinner on her way home.

Of course, she had texted Theo before she left town. A simple *love you* was all. He didn't need any tips or threats or admonishments. He was good. Too good, maybe.

Her GPS told Becky that it would take her four hours and twenty-eight minutes to get from Notre Dame to Hickory Grove. She told herself it wasn't bad. She could make it. The thought of staying the night alone in a motel room near Theo but not with him nearly gave her a stomachache. She had to get somewhere. To someone.

Once she hit the highway, she dialed Memaw.

"Hey, honey pie," the old woman answered. Her twang pulled Becky miles closer to home. Again, she pushed her fingers into her eyes. *It's a good thing. It's good. It's good. It's good*, she told herself as she took several deep breaths before replying.

"Sorry Memaw, bad connection." Becky's voice broke off. She swallowed, and opened her nostrils, and breathed in and out, ready to make another go of it before giving up and ending the call, but Grandbern's voice came over the line.

"Stop fussin', Faithy," he reprimanded his wife. Becky smiled, picturing the scene now. Cranky Grandbern and well-meaning Memaw arguing over how to hold the phone or where precisely to stand or sit as they spoke to her. "Rebecca? Do you have a full tank of gas?"

Becky licked her lips and felt the last of her tears glide down her throat and past her chest. "Yes, Grandbern. Well, no. I have three-quarters."

"How's the air in your tires?"

"I think it's fine."

Another squabble broke out in the distance of the call before Memaw took over. "We are so excited you're coming back, Rebecca Marie. I'm about to put a pie in the oven. Two pitchers of sweet tea. A loaf of cornbread. We're all ready for you. Do you need any shampoo, darlin'?"

***

Five hours later, Becky had finally made it off the highway and onto Main Street, the fat artery in town. If you stayed on it, it would take you right down past the Ohio River and straight into Louisville not twenty minutes later. In fact, the weather app on a smartphone would read the stats for Kentucky, rather than Indiana. They were that close.

All her childhood, there were competing notions about whether to call the area that split across the river Indiucky or Kentuckiana. Those conversations only ever took place on the evening news or among travelers from other states. As for Hickory Grove folks, it was just plain Hickory Grove, an almost-southern region of the U.S. of A.

Never once having returned home during her entire adulthood, Becky braced herself for dramatic changes. Maybe a new shopping plaza cropped up just outside of town. Maybe a few chain restaurants. Maybe there were fewer dirt roads and more traffic lights.

In fact, it was mostly the same. Hickory Grove was frozen in time. She drifted down the hill to the four-way stop. Downtown. A packed set of businesses leaned in across Main Street. The bank. The general store. A few others.

There, you could either turn left toward the old schoolhouse, right toward the firehouse, or straight on toward the farm.

With no other cars in sight, Becky rubbed her eyes hard and stared out her open window to see if the corner store had received a much-needed facelift in the time since she'd been gone. It was too dark to tell.

But what she could see was a silver truck parked in the gas station bay. Beyond the truck, facing the store as he pumped gas, stood a tall, blond man, wearing a t-shirt and jeans. Becky's stomach tightened and she bit her lip, recalling the boy she'd left behind all those years ago.

But it couldn't be. He'd left town when she had.

She put her foot on the gas and accelerated down Main Street.

***

Pulling up to the farm brought on a new set of emotions. Her mom wouldn't be there, of course. She was living the highlife with Randy out in California. They'd moved as soon as Becky and Ben graduated. Becky didn't hold it against her. She deserved to have fun and be happy. After so many years of waitressing and being a mom, Patsy Linden needed a break. She deserved it.

The headlights of the yellow truck washed over the dirt driveway and settled on the Linden family farmhouse. She parked and killed the engine. Dim porch lights took over and glowed above a precious picture.

Sitting in wooden rocking chairs out on the deck were Grandbern and Memaw. Different, also just the same.

Becky didn't bother with her bags. She stretched up from her truck and crossed in front of it, meeting Memaw in a big bear hug while Grandbern stayed behind in his seat.

"I missed you, girl," Memaw whispered into Becky's ear. Tears brimmed in her grandmother's paper-thin eyelids, but Becky smiled.

"I'm home now, Memaw. And I bet you'll get sick of me real fast." The two laughed and sniffled and walked up the steps. Grandbern opened his arms from the rocking chair, taking Becky into a firmer hug than she expected.

He wasn't well.

Her mother had told her this over the phone months ago, before Becky had decided what she was going to do once Theo left for college. Grandbern was old and cantankerous. His back hurt. He'd been having heart palpitations. Now, as he sat there in the rocking chair, Becky also noticed the tubes and the tank.

Under the milky yellow light of the porch lamp, Becky raised a finger and pointed to it. "What's up with the tank, Grandbern?"

"Aw, that ain't nothin' to worry about. Just gettin' old is all. Now Rebecca, I cain't remember. Is Theo playing ball for the Wildcats?"

It wasn't terrible. He wasn't so far off the mark. Three years ago, Theo was his high school's most promising pitcher. And lead-off batter. But between the school team and club and the personal trainer his father had hired, Theo burned out. It broke Becky's heart for her grandad, who always wished he could get off the farm as a boy to go play ball. She hoped he could watch Theo play someday. That never happened.

"No, Grandbern. He's at Notre Dame now. That's why I'm here. I just dropped him off today, remember?" She glanced up at Memaw who was clicking her tongue and shaking her head.

"Bernie, we went over this forty times. Rebecca is coming to live with us for a spell. Or maybe longer. Hopefully longer, in fact. Because I sure need someone else around here to help keep you on the straight and narrow." Memaw belted out a laugh. It startled Becky. So did the rhythmic, tired sighs from Grandbern's oxygen tank. Every tiny burst of air was an alarming interruption in their little reunion.

A dramatic change. Indeed.

Chapter 2: 1991

"You'll babysit in their homes." Patsy Linden (who had never married and swore she never would) spun six paper plates like Frisbees onto the farmhouse table. Anchored on one side by a long bench and the opposite by mismatched chairs, it served as the Linden Family meeting spot, homework zone, and meal central. No Linden was ever permitted to take breakfast, lunch, supper, or even a snack anywhere else. It had to be at the table.

But that didn't make their dinners formal.

Becky looked up at her mom from her place under the window. A fresh notebook page stretched in front of her and a newly sharpened pencil hovered above the pale blue lines. Dollar store stickers, still in their wrapper, framed the side of the page, ready for adornment.

"But if we're going to babysit as a real job, shouldn't we offer a—" she hesitated, racking her memory for that one word she'd overheard at the diner when an older local girl was planning her wedding. "Venue!" she cried out, taking to her notebook page in earnest.

Patsy cracked a tray of ice cubes then popped a couple into each of the eight plastic tumblers that lined the kitchen counter. "Venue? For *babysitting*?" She propped a hand on her slender hip and smirked at Maggie. The two shared a knowing expression, as though Maggie was a seasoned professional in the business world. As though *Patsy* were.

Becky made a face at Maggie, who'd begged to stay for supper. It was the first time in forever Patsy was home before eight, and she'd agreed to make her famous Mama's Mountain Mac. A backwoods take on crispy macaroni and cheese.

"I just think we have an opportunity, Mama. We could walk our charges to the schoolhouse and walk them home when their parents are back," Becky reasoned, having thought this through with great precision.

Patsy shook her head. "You'll probably babysit at night. Parents don't want their young children walking up Main Street or any other street after it gets dark. Keep the schoolhouse for your fort or whatnot."

Becky cringed. Having turned thirteen at the very start of summer, she was finally eligible to take the babysitting certification course that Hickory Grove Firehouse put on annually. Maggie had wanted no part until Becky reminded her that it was like a real job except you were the boss. Maggie liked that enough and followed along to the fire station, where they met two other girls from school: Kim Tremblay and Christie McGrath. Both girls were popular at Hickory Grove Middle, and Becky fully expected to be ignored during the CPR session and possibly teased during the session on the Heimlich maneuver.

Much to her surprise, both girls were kind. Their popular facade crumbled away as the new foursome took turns reading from a manual on changing diapers and then practicing together.

Once Becky and Maggie graduated (fully certified and available for hire), the question of business operations came up.

Dirk (Maggie's brother) and Ben teased the girls. Maggie's Aunt Lorna and Becky's mom offered lukewarm encouragement, asserting that *they* never took a babysitting certification class. The girls could tend children without it.

No one, however, realized how serious Becky was. Babysitting, for her, was part money-maker and part practice. If she had younger kids around, she could read stories to them and teach them all about her favorite books.

Everyone thought Becky ought to become a schoolteacher. After all, she almost always stayed after school to go help in the Kinder Garden at Hickory Grove Elementary. But Becky had no such intentions. Math, science and anything distinctly unrelated to the world of fiction served only to get her through school so that she could one day read for a living. And share her love of reading. She just wasn't sure how best to go about it.

Babysitting seemed like a good start. A captive (and impressionable) audience. No rigid lesson plans. No numbers. Perfect.

"The schoolhouse isn't a *fort*, Mom. Are you kidding me?" Becky felt herself grow hot.

Ben banged in through the screen door, tearing up the stairs as he hollered that he'd be down soon.

Patsy set the iced tea pitcher down with a purpose and pressed a hand to her forehead. "Let's just have a nice dinner for once. Okay, Rebecca? I'm never home. I don't want to put up with budding teenage attitude. I want to eat and laugh and smile and talk about anything and everything except money for once. Is that too much to ask?" Her voice rose into a crescendo and Maggie carefully backed away, falling onto the bench spot across from Becky, who had dropped her pencil and laid her head on the table.

"Fort? As in a children's play fort?" Grandbern had hobbled in from his recliner in the living room. He typically worked from sunup to sun down, just like any old-timey grandad who lived off of his own land. The day before, however, he'd fallen off a six foot ladder. Ice and ibuprofen had done nothing to ease his lower back pain. Becky's face fell at his unusually slow pace.

She opened her mouth to answer him, but thought better of it. Instead, she gave Maggie a meaningful look and jutted her chin to the right so Maggie would scoot down on the bench and make way for Grandbern.

"Daddy, I know it's not a fort. But to the girls, it's a play house. They're talking about cleaning it up and babysitting town children in it, like a daycare or something. A summer camp for reading. I just don't see how they're going to gain customers with such a crazy idea. That's all. I didn't mean to put it down."

Grandbern eased himself across from Becky and winked at her. "I think it's a right fine idea, Patricia. Rebecca, Maggie?" The girls snapped their heads to attention before he went on, ignoring his daughter's condescension. "Go on ahead. That old place could use a once-over. Just check in with the owners first, okay?"

Becky frowned. "Who owns it?"

Patsy joined them at the table, first calling out for Memaw and Ben to come down for supper, then answering Becky with a heavy sigh. "Hickory Grove Unified School District, of course."

"Really?" Maggie chimed in. "But it's not like… a real school."

Grandbern's upper lip snarled at the well-meaning remark and he twisted to their guest. "Young lady, it's as real a school as any. I learned my arithmetic and alphabet there just the same as you learned yours at your'n school up yonder hill there. 'Less a'course you went to school in some holler log." When Grandbern got agitated, his dialect flowed thicker than molasses.

Maggie shrunk down, avoiding his gaze and scooching closer to Becky's mom. Becky cut in. "Maggie just means that no one goes to school there anymore, Grandbern. It's abandoned now."

He nodded his head and pulled a plastic tumbler to his mouth, taking a long, silent sip, before setting it down, wiping his mouth with the back of his hand and turning his full attention to the baked macaroni dish that sat steaming in the middle of the table. "Eat first, talk later," he grunted and began doling out servings to each paper plate. By the time Ben and Memaw had joined them and grace had been said, Grandbern had one more thing to add. "It could be a real school if you two fixed it up and did your babysittin' business there, you know."

And that was all the momentum Becky needed. She made a note under "Venue" on her fresh page: *Call H.G. School District.*

***

No one answered the phone the next day. Becky and Maggie (well, mostly Becky) had called the district office five times to no avail.

"It's summer," Memaw offered after the sixth and final attempt. The three girls were sitting across the sofa in the living room. Memaw had her crochet work on her lap. Patsy was at the diner for a double shift. Grandbern was mowing. Ben was out riding his bike with Dirk.

"I've seen people working at the school in summertime. Like janitors and stuff. Someone has to be around," Becky whined. Maggie nodded sympathetically before clicking on the television set to find only three channels—all local. She gave up and clicked off before sauntering into the kitchen to rummage in the fridge.

"Why don't you all work on your advertisements in the meantime?" Memaw suggested.

Becky sank further into the couch cushions. It might just be time to give up. Her mom was right anyhow. No one would want their kids babysat in an abandoned building. It was a weird idea. Becky was weird. Too obsessed with books. If she wasn't careful, she'd embarrass herself. People would start talking about the girl who took children to the abandoned schoolhouse.

Total weirdo.

The screen door slapped open, and Grandbern stood in the frame, wiping his head with his handkerchief eyeing his wife and granddaughter. "What's wrong?" he asked, cranky as all get-out.

Memaw answered for them. "Becky and Maggie can't get ahold of anyone up at the school. They want permission to use the schoolhouse for their babysitting business."

Grandbern frowned in reply. "Permission, huh?" He crossed into the modest living room, taking a seat on a wobbly piano stool. "I'll give you the permission you need."

Becky's eyes lit up and she sucked herself out of the pillowy sofa, leaning onto her knees. "You can do that?"

"It's an abandoned building, ain't it?" he asked. "That ol' school district is probably just waiting for someone to come along and decide what in the world to do with it. Someone to clean it up for them. They ain't got the time or interest. You do it. I say you get yourselves over there soon as you can and get to work. Waiting won't change a thing. You'll do it or you won't. Don't wait on people to tell you what you can or cain't do it."

Becky cried out to the kitchen for Maggie to come hear the good news. They had their venue. Now they just needed to clean.

***

A limp rag hung from her hand while a half-full bucket of soapy water stood at her side. Becky had given Maggie the task of rounding up every single book she owned and could escape her house with (no one in Maggie's family would likely notice a missing book, assuming they had any at all).

Meanwhile, Becky turned up at the schoolhouse with her supplies. She just wasn't sure where to start. She had no desire to redecorate the place. Its allure to her was its age and weathered look. And she wasn't quite sure how much cleaning she ought to do. She didn't want to damage the wood or blackboards.

She dropped the wet rag into the bucket and returned to her broom, deciding to stick to the very basics for now while she brainstormed ideas for the business.

Her mom was right. Babysitting at the schoolhouse wouldn't go over well with Hickory Grove moms. Even the most lenient or absentee moms. So, instead, she and Maggie would offer a half-day camp for school children twelve and under. They would practice their reading and have one recess. No math. Five dollars per kid per day. Cash only.

Just as she bent over to grab the dustpan, the sound of bike tires on patchy gravel called her attention to the open doorway. Thinking it might be Maggie, Becky walked to the door and began to holler that she was inside.

Instead, it was her brother and a train of thirteen-year-old boys on bicycles, circling the schoolhouse like vultures.

"Playing house still, Becky?" Kevin Overgaard snorted. Becky's cheeks burned, and she glared at him before turning her head to her brother, awaiting his defense. When none came, she dropped the dustpan and her head then turned to go back inside.

"He's just joking, Beck," Ben called out, laughter filling his voice. Becky loved her brother. And he loved her. But they weren't friends. She turned, ready with a lame reply, when her eye caught one of the boys.

Zack Durbin.

Grandbern had warned them about the new family. A man and his son. New to town. New people didn't fare well in Hickory Grove. No one trusted their motives.

"They aren't new," Memaw had chided. "Durbins lived here years ago. These two just found their way home is all." No one had listened.

The dad was a lawyer. He practiced family and criminal law. Grandbern didn't trust lawyers and told Ben it was never wise to make friends with someone who was liable to sue you for looking at him wrong.

As far as Becky knew, this was Zack's first time playing with kids in town. *He picked the wrong crowd*, she secretly thought. Then again, Ben and Dirk and their friends weren't bad looking kids. But Zack was sure to be the cutest boy at school come September.

Becky suddenly grew aware of her frumpy outfit. Paint clothes. That's what her family called what she was wearing. Bleach stains and actual chunks of dried paint bent her t-shirt in odd angles. Too-long denim shorts folded unevenly on her unshaven thighs (she wasn't allowed to shave above her knees yet). Winnie the Pooh socks rolled haphazardly up her shins. She felt herself blush even harder, and she looked away from the blonde, blue-eyed specimen of an adolescent.

The boys took off up the road, and Becky turned to trudge back inside the schoolhouse. But a quiet voice lifted on the breeze behind her. "Cool place," Zack said.

She glanced back at him. A smile broke out on both their faces. And then, just as strangely as he'd turned up, he sped off. Dust billowed behind his bike as Becky watched on. A sigh escaped her lips, and she began to wonder if running a day camp was really how she wanted to spend her summer after all.

Chapter 3

Adding the hyphen should have been her clue. It wasn't so much the hyphen's fault. And she surely didn't think all women who hyphenated their last names *weren't in* love with the man whose name would come after that dang hyphen. But Becky wasn't the sort. She wasn't the sort to hyphenate. When it occurred to her back then, in 2000, that she'd better hang on to Linden, just in case . . . well, that was the beginning of the end.

"Need any more hangers?" Memaw's voice, somehow fragile now, wafted through the doorway. Becky set down the chintzy dollar-store photo album, smiled wanly at her grandmother, and then shook her head. A pile of all her entire wardrobe sagged on the bed behind her.

Memaw stepped into the bedroom, her paper-skinned hands neatly folded in front of her as she joined Becky at the dresser. "When your mama sent those photos, I knew something wasn't right."

Becky frowned in reply before laying a protective palm over the little album. Her wedding album. Four-by-six photos tucked carefully into plastic sleeves. Her mother's own photographs of the ceremony. None from the professionals. Those didn't come until months later. By the time they did, Becky wasn't sure she wanted them anymore. "What do you mean, Memaw?"

"I never did meet Andrew, and I'm not one to judge a book by his cover. But it didn't seem right, Becky. Just didn't."

Had Memaw admitted this before the wedding, it would have done little to change Becky's mind. She was set on marriage. On moving on. With someone who was different. Someone who would never remind her of *him*.

"Andrew wasn't a bad guy, Memaw. Still isn't." She forced down a laugh at that. Of course, her ex-husband was not a *bad* guy. He wasn't much of anything, in fact. He finished his degree, though. Which was more than Becky could say for herself. He had a good job as a manager somewhere, though she'd lost track by now. He eventually bought a three-bedroom, two-bath house in the suburbs of Tucson. Just as soon as he didn't have to share a mortgage with her. Or anything else for that matter.

Becky had always harbored a sneaking suspicion that Andrew hoped she'd run off with Theo so he could live his boring life alone. But he didn't say as much in the proceedings. The plan was vanilla. Standard. Theo lived with Becky full-time. He visited Andrew every other weekend and sometimes holidays or birthdays, though Andrew didn't put up much of a fuss.

Frankly, she wished he had. A little fire might have been enough to rekindle something for them. But once it was settled, reality set in. Becky was a twenty-two-year old single mother, alone in her new city. The city where she'd started college, only to quit once she fell under the spell of the first man she'd met. Homemaker. Stay-at-home mom. She'd given up her dream for Andrew, but Theo soon filled the void.

Besides, having a young child meant she could visit the library every single day. She even began volunteering for story time and headed the Sonoran Library's first Book Babes Book Club for Women Only. She liked the long title. And the exclusivity. It healed her. At least, it healed a part of her.

But volunteering didn't pay the bills any more than Andrew's piddly squat child support. She might have returned to finish her Library Science degree if it weren't for her hostage situation with daycares. She couldn't afford a nanny or au pair, so her only opportunity to make money was between the hours of eight a.m. and five p.m., Monday through Friday. Online classes scared her. And anyway, she was separated from Theo all day every day. She couldn't bear to prop him in front of the television set so she could advance an education which would likely never result in a job.

She'd have asked her mother to come live with her, if her mother hadn't gone back on her promises and run away to California with *Randy*.

Patsy claimed she'd never remarry. Maybe they never did get married. Becky didn't know if she'd live to learn the truth. Her mother was a different person, fulfilling her own lost youth with a man who never had children nor wanted them. Oh well.

"Your heart was always here, Rebecca Marie," Memaw whispered as she reached for the photo album and fanned through the pages. Why had the old woman left this in Becky's room? Becky didn't ask, instead taking the album from Memaw and tossing it into the trash at the base of the dresser. Memaw gasped. "You're going to throw it all away?"

Becky stared hard at the woman. "I threw that marriage away years ago."

Memaw giggled. A genuinely girlish giggle which escalated into loud cackles. Tears filled the crevasses on her cheeks, and she pressed her hands up to clear them away from beneath her glasses. "What?" Becky demanded. "What's so funny?"

"I don't mean the marriage, I mean the cheap photo album!"

"I know what you meant!" Becky's entire body relaxed and she let herself join in the laughter. But the laughing soon turned to crying as Becky finally let out over eighteen years of heartache and personal disappointment.

Memaw's smile faded and she pulled Becky in for a hug, her strength surprising for such a frail woman. "Rebecca. Becky," Memaw spoke close against her granddaughter's face, shushing her before forging ahead. "I know you wished we were there for your wedding. All I can say is that I'm sorry about that."

Becky's sobs tapered off and she gently pressed back, reading Memaw's face. A younger Becky would have waved away such an apology. Discounted her own need for it. Discounted anyone's wrongdoing. Least of all Memaw's. But she was a woman now. A woman who spent a lifetime—literally, the span between the birth and coming-of-age of her son—*being* the apology. Accepting none. Offering them all.

Sorry she didn't have a dedicated husband to take her out for a nice meal. Sorry she didn't have a mother to come pick Theo up from school when she was running late because of her first-ever kidney stone. Sorry she didn't live closer to family who could lift some of her burden. Sorry she'd ever left Indiana for the oven that was Arizona.

Of course, she was never sorry for Theo.

But now she drank in Memaw's apology as though it was the only thing that could quench her thirst. After all, Memaw was the Linden family matriarch. She had the power to apologize on behalf of her own daughter as much as Becky had the power to apologize on behalf of Theo that time he threw a baseball right through their neighbor's car. It was any wonder the neighbor even caught him, being that there were over a dozen kids playing ball in the dirt lot behind their apartment complex.

"Thanks for saying that, Memaw. It's been a hard while. It has. But I wouldn't change a thing. I'm here now. I'm still young enough to enjoy myself a bit. Which brings me to my next question."

"Shoot, girl," the old woman replied, repositioning her glasses on the bridge of her nose and running her hands down her cotton pants.

"Do you have cable yet? I'm only about four seasons behind on *The Golden Girls*."

***

When the doorbell chimed through the house, Becky raced out to it, nearly knocking Grandbern to the ground as he shuffled from the hallway to the living room.

It was Maggie. Her very best friend in the whole world since they were knee-high to a grasshopper, as Great Aunt Lorna would say.

Despite Maggie's monotonously shameless selfies from social media, Becky had clung to her own mental images of Maggie from childhood on up through high school.

Once Maggie texted her that she was heading over, Becky threw on lip-gloss and shook out her hair. She wanted her best friend to see her as Becky. Not Theo's mom. Not a loser divorcee who'd just road-tripped back home in pure desperation.

Like a cyber-gallery, she had revisited Maggie's different styles in her mind's eye.

Maggie as a little girl with her thatch of red bangs, cut by her own two hands on various occasions.

Maggie as a preteen, wearing her sweatshirt around her waist to hide her short shorts from "Lorna," who'd long given up the fight to keep "Aunt" in front of her name.

Maggie as a full-blown teenage babe, boldly opting for halter tops and forgoing her bangs in stark defiance. "Let them see my freckled forehead," she'd sung out while they were diving into ice cream one hot summer night. "I think it's sexier than Kim Tremblay's Cover Girl skin any day!"

Becky loved her friend's confidence. But sometimes it caused trouble for the teens. Particularly, once Maggie started dating seriously.

"Eek! It's you!" Maggie shrieked through the screen door. At first, Becky thought it was the hash marked screen that distorted her image. But then the recent selfies reminded her otherwise.

Gone were the bangs. Gone was the halter. Gone, too, was Maggie's red head.

"Blonde?" Becky squeaked at last. That was the best she could come up with for their reunion?

She opened the door carefully, as though a poorly behaved dog might wedged its way in. Maggie gripped the aluminum frame and tore it open from Becky, ignoring the shock that plastered her face. "Trust me, it's all a lie," Maggie replied, eyeing Becky with suspicion before continuing. "I've had *less* fun, if anything."

Becky laughed and looked past Maggie toward a dusty SUV cooking on the dirt drive. "Don't worry, they're home. It's just us girls."

"I thought I was going to get to meet them?"

"You're not leaving tonight, are you? You'll have plenty of time. And you'll regret you ever said as much. Four heathens is what they are. Animals. Luckily, Gretchen's boyfriend broke up with her, so all she has to do is sit on the sofa surfing the internet and taking downer selfies."

Becky smirked. She'd kept good track of Maggie's kids. Sending small gifts for every birthday and even Christmas. Sometimes just hard candy. Other times, a t-shirt. Gretchen was closest to Theo in age. Then Dakota. Ky. And finally Briar.

Almost too late, Becky stepped back from the door and waved Maggie in for a deep hug. She smelled just as Becky remembered, like dryer sheets. Not fresh laundry. Dryer sheets. She knew the difference because Maggie had admitted to using them as perfume when they were twelve.

Other than the blonde hair, nearly everything else about Maggie was the same. Pencil-thin eyebrows above bright, green eyes. Full, colorless lips. Her thin frame had filled out some, but her rhinestone-studded jeans and graphic tee complimented the new curves. Becky said so.

"Well, *you* look the exact same, Rebecca Marie Linden." She stood back from Becky and studied her from head to toe, offering a detailed commentary on Becky's distinct lack of gray hairs, her smooth skin, and, "Did you grow?"

"What do you mean?"

"You look taller."

Becky raised an eyebrow before waving Maggie back to her old bedroom, where she was in the middle of her third and final box. She'd packed light.

As soon as they were inside, Becky sank onto the bed, exhaustion suddenly overwhelming her. Maggie, however, got to work, digging through Becky's box like they were still in high school. Still sharing clothes, drinks, chapstick, and everything else that existed between two teenage girls. Becky started to inquire about Travis, but Maggie's face scrunched in disgust.

"First of all, I'm not talking about my derelict husband. Not on a Sunday. It's unholy. Second of all, I have one, big, fat, juicy question for you, and you know exactly what it is." Becky didn't. "Have you called Zack, yet?"

Chapter 4

No, she hadn't called *Zack*. How could she? He hated her. Once she tried to explain that to Maggie, her friend grew incredulous, citing the fact that he was still living in town and was still very *single*, as though it mattered.

It didn't. Zack was old news. A high school romance. Things ended amicably enough, despite Maggie's gossip in the aftermath. Despite the fact that no one came to Tucson for her wedding six months later, including Maggie. Despite a lot of facts, in fact.

But Becky was adult enough to ask her best friend how he was doing. What he was doing. Who he became after eighteen years.

Maggie had begun to hang up the sparse collection of blouses Becky unpacked.

By the time Becky opened her mouth to ask about her high school boyfriend, Maggie had moved on to complaining that Kim Tremblay bought the Haunted House at the top of Overlook Lane. Maggie was forever pining over the fabled Haunted House.

It wasn't *actually* a haunted house. It just looked like one. And its spot at the top of a long, jagged hill gave it a looming effect. The way cartoon haunted houses sort of lean into the television set like they might jump out of the screen and stab you with their steeples.

"You'll own that house one day, Mags. I promise," Becky assured her, knowing full well that Maggie, in debt to her ears and lawfully tied to the scum of the earth with four children at her ankles, hips, and shoulders, would never move out of the rusty little clapboard on Pine Tree Lane.

Maggie threw her head back and laughed. "Even if I had the money, no one is going to pay to live next to wacky old Fern. I'll never sell my house."

Becky's eyes grew wide. "So she's still there?" Fern Gale was a town legend in Hickory Grove. No one seemed to know where she came from or even how old she was. All they knew was she never took down her Christmas lights and preferred weeds and yard trash over, say, flowers or garden gnomes. Although, it was likely that there were many garden gnomes hidden in there somewhere. Everyone called it the Christmas House. A nickname far sweeter than the place deserved.

"You won't have to sell it if you win the lottery. You could just do that thing that millionaires and billionaires always do. A business foreclosure or whatever. Just give it up, you know."

Maggie eyed Becky mischievously. "Speaking of giving things up, let's return to my earlier question." Becky felt her nostrils flare and her mouth involuntarily twist into a grin. Her breath came easier and a giggle tickled her throat. Maggie noticed and egged her on. "Oh, yeah. That's what I'm talking about. You *do* want the scoop you little liar."

At that Becky's smile slipped. "It's just . . . complicated. I've moved so far from Hickory Grove, physically and emotionally. I can barely picture him anymore." Okay, *that* was a lie.

Maggie ignored it, racked the last hanger, swiveled on the ball of her bare foot and fell onto the bed like a thirteen-year-old again. Becky joined her, sliding down onto her pillow, taking note that it wore the same exact pillow case as it had when she left: a white slip with hand-embroidered rosebuds trailing into the corner.

"Spill," Becky commanded, feeling more herself than she had since she'd moved out to Arizona.

"Okay, sooo . . ." Maggie sat up like her spine had been sewn to a pole. Becky knew this posture well. Her friend meant business. "We have to start at the beginning. With your wedding."

Becky cringed. Meeting Andrew, falling into lust, agreeing to a shotgun wedding once her pregnancy proved real, and then giving up her degree all because of a careless first year. It really would be reasonable to say that marrying Andrew was the worst decision of her life.

But it wasn't. She got Theo out of the deal. So, technically, it was the best decision she ever made. It just happened to cost her in other areas of her life, like (for example) any hope of a quality romantic relationship.

"Zack heard about your wedding through Ben, naturally," Maggie forged ahead as Becky squeezed her eyes shut and began to massage her left temple. "Then Ben told us," her friend twirled a finger around as if to suggest she was part of the Linden brood. She was, really. "Zack was a real jerk about it. Pretending he didn't care and saying he had a girlfriend anyway."

Becky knew all this. Maggie had spilled it on the phone until she couldn't take it any longer, hanging up and instigating one of their longer periods of mutual silent treatment. Now, she opened her eyes and cautiously peered over to Maggie, unsure if her friend remembered that part. Crossed arms and a hyper-arched brow confirmed that she did.

"Sorry, Mags," Becky replied. "It was a really hard time for me. You know that."

Maggie nodded and sighed. "I know, Beck. But you could have moved home *then*. You could have lived with me or back here."

"No. I couldn't do that to Andrew *or* Theo. We got married in Tucson. We had Theo in Tucson. I was stuck. You can't just move states when you have a kid and a fragile custody arrangement."

"Why didn't you come back for a holiday? Or visit? Eighteen years is forever. You could have driven. Left Theo or brought him. Why didn't you?" Maggie's face softened. She was trying to understand. Or seemed to be.

Becky thought about it. It was the same question Memaw and Grandbern asked every time she spoke to them. Her rare communications with her mom and Ben didn't result in the same guilt-ridden pleading, which was why her phone calls to her grandparents drew rarer and briefer. Anyways, she always had go-to answers. *Soon.* And *Next year!* Or *I'm super busy, but I really want to!*

Flake. Becky knew she was a flake. And, also, when Ben had told her that Zack was dating, it sealed the deal. The door shut.

"I don't know, Mags. I wish I had. But I'm here now, right?"

Maggie shook her head. It wasn't enough. "Why didn't you call Zack?"

That one Becky had an answer for. "I didn't have his number anymore!"

"Psh, don't be ridiculous. If you think you're going to move back to Hickory Grove with a handful of college credits and a mouthful of excuses, then we don't want you. None of us." Maggie rose, catching Becky off-guard.

"Maggie, what are you talking about? You and I talk all the time. Letters. Facebook. Phone calls."

Maggie's body relaxed. She had clearly forgotten that she wasn't *actually* mad at Becky. "Yeah, I know. But it bothered some people that you didn't come back even for one Christmas."

Becky's face fell. She knew it bothered her grandparents. And the only other person who'd have cared was Mags. All she had in the world, other than Theo, were those three, and she had let them down. But, still, she reasoned, relationships were two-sided.

Becky really wanted to scream back, *You could have visited me! I needed you more! I had a child. Alone!* But she knew that no one could afford to travel across the country. How *she* had was a miracle. And besides, what good would it do? The past had to stay in the past. No sense in fueling the fire. Maggie was here now. Becky took a breath. "Fresh start. Okay?"

A grin spread over Maggie's mouth, and she nodded her head, blinking away the beginning of a tear. "In that case, let's get back to Zack."

If there was one thing that always made Maggie feel better, it was gossip. However, to Becky, Zack wasn't gossip. He was her history. And that thread of a conversation didn't help them start fresh. It was a rehashing of history. Still, Becky was desperate for details.

Maggie spent the next ten minutes solid recapping every single thing she could think of, and Margaret Eleanor Engel (formerly Devereux) could think of everything. Becky learned that Zack fell off the face of the earth for several years until he suddenly reappeared in Hickory Grove in 2004.

"No one even told me." Maggie's voice rose. An accusation against both Zack and his family. Had Maggie ever even met Zack's dad? No one seemed to have. His mother had died. That's as much as anyone knew—or claimed to. "Anyway," Maggie continued. "That's when it became clear that Zack had *not* followed in his father's footsteps after all."

Becky frowned. Zack had always told her he was going into education. He wanted to become a teacher or professor. Not a lawyer, like his own father. He thought lawyers were scumbags, even. "He never wanted to follow his dad's footsteps," she cut in.

Maggie rolled her eyes. "Guys like Zack *always* want to live up to their dad's expectations. It's one of the rules of life. If you're a guy, and your dad is sort of rich, then you take over whatever thing he does that makes him rich so that you can be rich and no one is upset or uncertain."

Becky thought about this. She couldn't picture Zack heading down to his father's office front on Main Street with its deceptively quaint sign declaring "Family Law." In fact, the one thing everyone *did* know about Mr. Durbin, Esquire, was that he was the man to visit if you were getting a divorce or had been "accused of" driving under the influence.

Most people hated him just by virtue of his job.

"Wait," Becky interrupted. "How do you know he didn't become a lawyer?"

Maggie stopped and looked at her, cocking her bleached hair to the side. "I figured you heard."

Becky shook her head lamely. She was firmly out of the loop. "Nope," she admitted.

Without skipping a beat, Maggie answered. "Zack works for the school now. Hickory Grove Unified School District. I think he's an administrator or something. Not a principal, but he's always at board meetings and Gretchen told me she saw him walking around the high school just last year."

A frown formed on Becky's face. For all the gossip in which Maggie loved to partake, she never paid attention to the important stuff. She missed deadlines on her electric bill every month, sometimes even paying the wrong amount through her banking app. She had little sense of direction outside of Hickory Grove, probably unsure whether New Albany was north, south, east, or west. And though she knew Zack got home each day before five p.m. and that he wore a suit and tie, she had no idea what his job was. Hadn't even bothered to perform a simple Google search. But if he *was* working at the school, then he'd done what he said he was going to do. He became a teacher.

Becky smiled.

Chapter 5

Maggie had to go. Gretchen called and said everyone was throwing up and she wasn't going to clean three trash cans worth of vomit. Irritated to core, Maggie spit curse words then promised Becky they'd meet back up for more dish.

As Becky walked her to the front porch, Maggie turned to add one last thing. "Listen, all you need to know for now, Beck, is that Zack is *here* and he is *single*. You do with that info what you will." The yellowy blonde floated out to her SUV and waved Becky off without looking. Dust kicked up under her SUV as Becky returned inside, overwhelmed by the prospect of finishing her unpacking.

"Rebecca." Grandbern's voice startled her from the living room recliner, his new perch, as Memaw called it. She turned and saw the old man sinking into his recliner, one hand gripping the remote, then other cupping his plastic tumbler and waving it toward her. "Sorry to interrupt, but could you fill 'er up?"

She smiled at him and did as he asked, heading to the kitchen to pour his umpteenth glass of sweet tea. When she returned, she pecked him on the cheek and fell into the couch nearby. "Faithy says she's going to pour sweet tea into my oxygen tank if I don't slow down," he whispered.

A laugh escaped Becky's mouth. "If she doesn't want you to drink so much sweet tea then why does she keep making it?"

"That just what I told her," he answered through the puffs of his tank. "She's a—whadda ya call it? An enabler." He turned his stare to the television, and hardness replaced the joke.

Becky wondered where he learned the word enabler. It wasn't that Grandbern was illiterate or stupid. On the contrary. He was the smartest man she knew, next to Theo. But his knowledge was rural in nature. And rural folk didn't use psychobabble, as her mother used to say. Enable and its derivatives being just that.

She lounged for a while, staring mindlessly at the baseball game. Grandbern had never watched television when she was home. She couldn't remember a single time he'd ever sat in front of a screen. She looked over at him and saw heaviness pull his eyes down and expected a light snoring to come next, but it didn't. Instead, more puffs from the tank. Becky pulled herself up from the couch, gave him another peck on the cheek, and returned to her bedroom to grab her shoes.

She needed a few staples. Namely popcorn, because Memaw had forgotten to stock it for Becky's re-entry. Also toothpaste, because she couldn't find her own and had noticed that all Memaw and Grandbern had were sample tubes from the dentist. Uncertain if they were emergency back-ups, she figured she could use a few other small things, anyway.

In her bedroom, she glanced at herself in the mirror above the dresser. She had managed to shower and wash her hair the night before. Now that she was back in Indiana, she didn't need a blow dryer to lift it out of its dry, limp state. The humidity gave Becky her old waves back, and a quick scrunch made the dirty blonde tresses passable.

For a shirt, Becky still had on her pajama tee, which was an old freebie someone in the house had gotten simply for being in the vicinity of a half marathon. Becky would never run a half marathon. Being raised on a farm taught you that real exercise happened naturally over the course of a day of hard work. Fake exercise was a waste of the time God gave you.

She looked down her legs at the cut-off sweats she wore when she cleaned. All she had to do was hit the corner market. Chances of running into anyone familiar were slim to none, especially on a Sunday morning in Hickory Grove, when everyone was at church, including Memaw.

Becky left her outfit as it was and shoved her feet into rubbery clogs she'd found at a dollar store a few months back. Then she grabbed her purse, which was actually a fanny pack that she disguised as a purse by slinging it over her shoulder and tucking it under her arm. She liked fanny packs, because they were small and practical. Sure, she had a real purse, but that was only for appearances.

Leafing through the minimal contents, she brushed past her credit card, which she reserved for big-ticket items, and found her stash of cash. She was down to forty-two dollars. Becky wondered if she ought to transfer banks this week but put the thought aside. She wouldn't need a bank until she had a job, which was another thought she pushed aside.

Considering her options, Becky decided against driving up to the store. Another car ride sounded like pure torture. She could walk, but that would take a little longer than she cared to leave Grandbern.

So, on a whim, she headed out to the barn, where she'd kept her bicycle as a teenager. Knowing Memaw and Grandbern, it had to be there. If her room was any indication, then they had gotten rid of exactly nothing in the interceding years.

Sure enough, right by the door, covered in a thick layer of dust and cobwebs, sat her cruiser. She'd gotten it second-hand for her sixteenth birthday. A bike was what the richest of the poor kids would get for a sixteenth birthday, and it had made her life at the time.

Becky glanced around the rest of the barn, noticing little had changed, indeed. More junk, to be sure. Definitely not less. Whatever she needed she would be able to find here. It gave her a comfort.

Before mounting the bike, she glanced around for a rag or towel and found a stack sitting on Grandbern's workbench. She grabbed one off the top and went to work wiping down her bike. It wasn't until she scrubbed at the seat that she realized the rag had some oil on it. But since she was wearing her cleaning shorts, it didn't matter.

She tossed the rag back and then assessed the tires. They weren't as flat as she'd expected, but they weren't ridable, either. Becky knew Grandbern hadn't thrown away his pump, but it was no longer sitting right there next to her bike. Then, she noticed that Ben's bike was also missing.

He had to have taken it. She let out a sigh, did a loop through the over-crowded barn, straining her eyes around cans and tools, lawn mowers, and junk, but she couldn't spot the pump. Knowing the corner market now had a gas station, she was certain it would also have a water and air station. The only thing to do was walk the bike all the way there.

Fastening her fanny pack around her waist, she then grabbed the handles and pushed the bike down the dirt-and-gravel drive and out onto Main.

On her walk, Becky inhaled the smell of the country. So different from the desert.

She had grown to love Tucson, especially at this time of year. Monsoons were a great shock that first summer. She thought it never rained in the desert. Counted on it, even, expecting to lay out on the quad in the warm sun. What she learned was that Tucson was all about extremes. At least in August. It was either an oven or a monsoon hit and you had to be wary of flash flooding.

Becky didn't mind it either way, really, and she loved the smell of rain in the desert. When the water hit the saguaros and trickled into the dirt, an earthy smell rose up from the ground and filled her lungs with more than a scent. It was a sensation. To bottle it would have held her through the hard months. Like the ninety-degree temperatures on Thanksgiving or the years she had switched out of her fleece leggings for shorts on Christmas.

But in Indiana, the earthy smell took on a different flavor. There was no way of describing it other than to say it smelled like home. The best smell.

After a while, Becky came upon the little cemetery at the corner of Overlook and Main. It had always reminded her of a t.v. show character's mouth, with teeth popping up from the grass at odd angles and sporadically.

She glanced at her watch as though time were of the essence then looking to the sky, inexplicably, for some kind of answer. The answer was, she decided, that she deserved a break. There was no rush to get to the store or to unpack or anything else. For the time being, she could explore a little. Smell the roses. All that.

So, she pushed the kickstand down and spent what felt like forever stabilizing her heavy bike before summiting the small hill where a few of her ancestors had been laid to rest decades upon decades ago.

She wove through the sparse stones, reading off familiar names and squinting through the mossy overgrowth to examine dates.

Finally, when she had read nearly every single tombstone, she stood at the far end and stared over the land. Rolling hills of green lapped into each other like waves in the ocean, not that she'd ever been to the ocean, but she was sure this is what it looked like. Just blue instead of green.

Her eyes caught on the same exact buildings that existed before she left and a conflict rose in her. Part of her wished Hickory Grove would grow and catch up with the times. The other part was grateful it hadn't.

Then, just as she dropped her hands from her waist to head back down to her bike, she saw it. In the distance, where it had always sat among hills and away from everywhere.

The one-room schoolhouse.

***

Not ten minutes later, she was propping her bike against its fading white siding.

Becky glanced around it, amazed to see no real differences in the landscape or surrounding area. Hickory Grove, though small in population, was an expansive town set in miles of grassy meadows and rolling mounds of rye.

An image of Grandbern popped in her head. A little-boy version of Grandbern. In a black-and-white outfit holding a tin pail.

Becky frowned. How old was Grandbern? She'd sent a card and a small package of his favorite candy (Red Tamales) for his eightieth birthday which had to have been at least two years ago— probably longer—because Theo wasn't driving yet (or else she'd have sent *him* to the post office). The postal worker had struggled with the zip code. Becky remembered all this because she'd called up Memaw and Grandbern to warn them that he may never receive the best present of his life. They laughed.

If Grandbern were 83 or so, then he was born in 1936, which put him at the school in the 1940s and 50s, which was relatively late for schoolhouses, wasn't it? Maybe not. At least, not in rural America, with its desperation to stay old. Then again, it probably didn't have a choice in the matter.

Despite the warmth of the late morning, Becky's skin turned to gooseflesh as she began to circle the house, examining its exterior like she was an insurance adjuster. She wondered if it had always been in this bad of shape. The foundation seemed non-existent as though the earth had begun to swallow the building down. Moss crawled up and into soft-looking corners. The roof, in one area, was sinking, too. Becky stepped back and circled a second time, now noticing that Sleepy Beauty-esque vines that had begun their thorny ascent. Mother Nature's claws.

She wondered if it was the circle of life. If the schoolhouse was beginning to fade away much like the children who'd once attended. Becky shook away the thought, knowing full-well that this place would never disappear. It was a monument to a forgone time. A relic. History's offspring.

Bypassing the rotted wooden steps at the front, Becky walked to the back entrance now, whose door stood firmly against the test of time but whose stoop had all but disappeared. It didn't matter much, as the entire back side was slumping so low that the threshold nearly met with the ground.

Once inside, she breathed in the earthen smell and knew that, no, the schoolhouse hadn't changed so much. What surprised Becky the most was the distinct lack of *peopleness* inside. After all, she and Maggie practically *lived* there in the 1980s and 1990s. No one had bothered to ransack the place.

The very same graffiti that she recalled as a child was still in its place, if not more faded or covered in dust or foliage now.

But that was it.

Her relief was tempered by a degree of defensiveness. It seemed like there hadn't been a single soul—not in *eighteen* years—who was fascinated enough to journey off the road and into the alluring little building that had begun to sink into the hills of Hickory Grove.

Their loss, she thought and slid one foot after another around the small space. Small, indeed. It seemed like the room had shrunk in. Perhaps it *had*.

One thing Becky knew for sure was different. It was dirtier than a groundhog's den. All her hard work—her sweeping and wiping and polishing—had meant nothing now. Her mother would be so mad to know she'd wasted good furniture polish only for the dust to multiply a million-fold in nothing but an old abandoned building.

But wasn't that what cleaning was, anyway? A temporary endeavor? Only to be undermined by the passage of time?

Anyway, the schoolhouse didn't quite count as an abandoned building. Becky had never abandoned it.

She traced a finger along the teacher's desktop, recalling some of the books that she'd stacked there, playing librarian.

Now, in that moment, she briefly considered going back to school. She could get her degree finally. Become what she'd always wanted to be.

The thought washed away as Becky left the desk and moved toward the little wood-burning stove in the center of the room. *Could it still be there*? No way. Someone had surely scavenged the old, brittle firewood long before it had ever rotted, probably.

She squeezed her eyes shut and pictured the knobby chunk of oak. The inscription he'd scratched into it. A promise. A teenager promise. Their initials. A heart, hugging the B and Z together.

She opened her eyes and looked down at the stove top. Becky was right.

Someone had taken it.

Chapter 6: 1992

The math class incident.

That's what Maggie and Becky decided to call it. The moment when, in algebra class, Becky plopped down next to Zachary Durbin.

The same boy who, despite being athletic and hot and cool, had his pencil poised directly above a fresh piece of line notebook paper with his name already scrawled in the upper left-hand corner. On the first day of high school. Alone in a corner seat in a math class.

New kids were weird.

For some reason, Becky did not expect such a specimen to partake in the day-to-day of high school life. Before school had even started, a rumor began to swirl that the NFL was scouting him. Becky always questioned this, as she couldn't quite picture serious NFL people hunched over the creaky bleachers out at Hickory Grove Middle School during the high school's summer football practices.

Still, Zack checked off all the boxes. Tall, blonde, tanned, muscular beyond his years. Everyone took an interest in him the minute his family moved to town. A little pride flickered in her chest at the realization that this cool new boy had chosen *her* brother as one of his first friends.

Sitting next to Zack happened quite by accident. She'd simply wanted to be near Maggie, and the only available spot was behind Maggie and on the inside of him. Becky had no choice.

He caught her gaze and smiled widely, unaware of the breech in cool-kid procedure.

Unconvinced that he was actually smiling at her, she flashed a nervous grin then turned her attention to the teacher and pretended to care about numbers.

An hour later, Mr. Powell called on Zack to work a problem on the chalkboard.

He solved the equation seamlessly then nodded to a pleased Mr. Powell who dismissed him to sit back down. The rest of class sat star struck. The new kid was an enigma. Brawny and brainy. A bizarre combination.

Becky's eyes followed Zack the whole time. A crisp, blue polo fit his torso just so. Jean shorts hit his knees above clean, white socks and Nike tennis shoes.

Her gaze dropped to her own outfit. She'd dressed as trendy as possible for the first day, taking Maggie's advice and doing with it what she could under a thrift-shop budget.

A too-tight tank top hugged her adolescent body. Her second-hand denim shorts rose high on unshaven thighs. Becky was only allowed to shave up to her knee. Good thing she had sparse, blonde leg hair. She pulled her newly assigned textbook onto her lap and pressed her knobby knees together as close as she could get them.

Once Zack rounded the last row of desks and began his walk back to his seat, he kept his gaze on her, a smile pulling at the corners of his mouth. Becky could hardly hear anything through the pounding of her heart. Not Mr. Powell's next set of directions. Not the rest of the class murmuring after Zack's performance. Only the throbbing of blood in her ears.

Then, just as he pressed his hands down on his desktop to ease into the seat, Zack Durbin winked at her.

Winked. At. Her.

It was the first time a guy had ever winked at Becky Linden. It might have even been the last. She could have fallen out of her seat right then and there, but that would be an overreaction. She sucked in a breath and wondered if she ought to wink back.

Hero that he was, Mr. Powell saved her, dismissing them thirty seconds before the bell. She opened her mouth to say something to Zack . . . to save the moment. Extend it. But Maggie whipped around. "Bathroom, now!"

Zack smiled at both girls, his eyes lingering on Becky before Maggie tugged her from the room, totally oblivious to a real-life, love-at-first-sight experience.

Becky tried to explain this to her best friend once they were safely in front of a girls' room mirror, where Maggie could apply four coats of lip gloss and one extra coat of mascara. After Maggie's initial "Eek!" She spit the cold, hard truth back at Becky. "But it's not love at first sight, Beck. He's Ben's friend. You saw him before."

Maggie was right, if a little slow on the uptake.

Who cared if they had seen each other *one* other time? That happened earlier in the summer. They were children then. Now, they were high schoolers. And they were sitting directly next to each other in math class. It was positively love at first sight.

"Doesn't Grandbern hate him?" Maggie pressed.

Grandbern hated *lawyers*. He wouldn't hate Zack. The problem was, however, that Zack Durbin's dad was the lawyeriest of lawyers in the greater George County area. His brief time in town had proven as much. Reputations spread like wildfire in Hickory Grove, and Lawyer Durbin wasn't faring well.

So, yes. There was a high probability that Grandbern *might* hate Zack by extension.

None of that mattered, however, when Zack showed up at the farm the next weekend, a bouquet of carnations in hand, to request a meeting with Rebecca Linden's parents.

Chapter 7

She forced herself to leave the school and climb back up the hill, pushing her rusty bike with its deflated tires and her rusty body with its deflated heart.

By the time Becky reached the corner of Main Street and Overlook Lane, she'd worked herself into an Indiana sweat.

An Indiana sweat was different from an Arizona sweat.

In Arizona, it was so hot and dry, that your body cooked like overdone scrambled eggs. Its top layer turned to a golden crust. All your moisture evaporated away until your body was so charred that it panicked and sent its last reserves to its important zones- your spine and your cleavage, namely. Whoever coined the tasteless term "boob sweat" was likely from Arizona. And then there was the Arizona-Sweat Smell. Even if you were just walking from your car into the grocery store, you began to smell like you'd been working on a car engine for two days straight without a break.

In Indiana, the sweat was half yours and half the atmosphere's. A mixture of sweet humidity and your own beadlets settled everywhere, evenly, leaving no hot spots or puddles. Just a layer of moisture that someone might mistake for cleverly applied highlighter.

It occurred to Becky that this was the first hint of exercise she'd had in years. Shame might have kicked in if she didn't feel so darn good. She silently resolved to walk every single day from now until forever.

After some time, she arrived at the market but paused before entering. The place was dead, as she'd predicted. A quiet utterance of gratitude escaped her mouth and she contemplated whether to fill her tires first or shop first. Opting for the latter, in order to give herself a small break from manual labor, she propped the bike against the side of the building and rounded the corner to the store front.

Once inside the modest shop, Becky nodded at the cashier, an unfamiliar face who didn't bother to look up. It was just as well. She'd be in and out. No time for conversation. She had bare essentials to tote home.

First up on her mental checklist: toothpaste. Becky made her way to the personal care section which happened to sit at the end of the canned food aisle. After grabbing the cheapest tube, her eye caught a sale on deodorant.

Becky wasn't one to buy something simply because it was on sale. That was the first rule of being frugal. You bought something because you desperately needed it, not because it was a dollar cheaper than usual. Some people thought frugal meant shopping sales. Becky knew better.

Still, this particular brand of deodorant was half off (*half off!*), so she scooped up the stick in front and made a little show of double-checking the label (a good deodorant doubled as an antiperspirant, of course).

Satisfied but still focusing down on the plastic hygienic product, she turned to head up the aisle for the rest of her supplies.

Not two steps later, her peripheral vision caught sight of someone looming at the end of the aisle. Becky nearly dropped her stick of deodorant and tube of toothpaste. Her mouth fell open and she glanced around, panicked.

He hadn't seen her yet. She still had time to twist around and dash the other way. And that's exactly what she did, until . . .

"*Becky?* Is that you? *Becky Linden?*"

Inexplicably, Becky turned and corrected him. "It's Linden-Spaur now." A lump formed in her throat and she locked eyes with none other than Zack Durbin.

He hesitated, giving her time to do two things: freak out over her outfit, mussed hair, bare face, and that pesky layer of sweat that had receded to her hairline which no doubt added a lovely greasy effect. Also, she took him in. He was wearing jeans and a t-shirt and had decided not to grow old but to grow up.

Men and women like that fascinated Becky. They improved over time, not like wine (that metaphor always irritated her for some reason), but like . . . well like attractive people just tend to do. His shirt cut across his chest beautifully. A full head of hair set in place above kind eyes and nothing more than well-earned crow's feet.

Jealousy kicked at her stomach. Who had he been laughing with for nearly twenty years? She checked his left hand.

No ring.

That's right. Maggie had said as much.

"Oh, I'm sorry," he answered, a smile dancing over his lips. *What did she say?* Becky felt like she'd lost track of an hour. Oh yeah. Linden-Spaur. Just perfect. She tucked the unsightly deodorant under her arm and smoothed her paint shirt down as best she could, sucking in her stomach and leveling her jawline to avoid any hint of a double chin.

Composure was everything. She had to recover. Somehow. "Well, I haven't dropped the Spaur yet."

Oof. She winced. Zack frowned in reply. "Oh, well. I'm sorry again, in that case." His hand raised to the back of his head and he glanced behind himself toward the cashier. He was trying to get out of it. She could tell. He took one look at her and regretted everything. *Jerk. Was he always such a jerk?*

But then, he took a step closer to her. "Becky, what are you doing in town?"

She raised her eyebrows, unprepared to keep up the facade that they were old friends rather than first loves. The facade that they hadn't broken each other's hearts.

Shifting her weight, Becky answered, "I'm back now. My, um, my son is in college. Up north at Notre Dame. So, I'm back."

Slowly, Zack nodded his head. Becky might look like a homeless person, but at least her son's education had some value. She swallowed and looked away, her eyes taking in the progression from shampoo to canned chicken.

"Notre Dame, eh?" Yep, she was right. It would save her for the moment. Becky made a promise right then and there to burn this outfit. Zack took another step toward her. They were now only about two feet apart. Could he smell her? Would he smell the Arizona sweat or the Indiana glow? Would he catch sight of the deodorant and nod his head solemnly? Maybe point at it and remark that it was a smart purchase?

Realizing he sort of asked a question, she mustered up an answer. "Yeah. Engineering. Maybe." She should definitely ask him about himself. But what would she say? *Did you get over me?* Or maybe: *Do you hate me?* Of course she could simply ask him how he'd been.

"How've *you* been, Zack?" Her overemphasis on the *you* came across snarky. She opened her mouth to try again but he ignored it and answered through a sigh.

"Good, real good. Just working, you know. I've been back since I graduated." He chuckled. "I guess you really can't take the small town out of the boy or however that saying goes."

Becky smiled. Zack was smart, no doubt. But she'd always rolled her eyes at his clichés. Even when they were together in high school he would say things like "What doesn't kill you makes you stronger" and "It is what it is." She supposed this one wasn't as egregious. She supposed none of them were. Maybe she liked that about Zack. His little one-liners added a softness to the former high school athlete. The current bachelor. Apparently.

He scratched his head again but stayed in place. Becky wondered where this could possibly go. He looked so good. She looked so miserable. There was no way she could stand to stay in Hickory Grove if she was going to run into Zack Durbin on a regular basis. It was painfully awkward. She tucked the deodorant more deeply under her arm and then began to wave the tube of toothpaste in goodbye, but he cleared his throat. "Do you need to be somewhere?"

Becky blinked. "I need to fill my bike tires with air."

"I can help," he offered, stepping back and sweeping his hand for her to pass. But there was no way she was going to let him walk behind her and get a full, unabashed view of what he was *no longer* missing.

Awkwardly, she waved her hand, too. "Oh, thanks, that'd be okay."

A half smile pulled at his mouth and he nodded his head. Side by side, they walked up to the cashier. She decided on the spot to forgo the rest of her list. The only thing that made deodorant-buying worse was when you bought it with one random food item. It was best to keep hygiene products separate from food products.

Maybe she ought to mention that to the manager of the store one day.

***

Outside, in the late-morning sun, she felt more comfortable and less comfortable all at once. In the sun, she was more exposed. He might even be able to see her love handles through the paint shirt. But, she also knew the sun brought out her freckles and the golden streaks in her hair. The light would brighten her eyes and glow across her skin.

Zack offered to take over, and Becky let him, admiring the view as he worked the little tire caps off and filled each tire over the vibrating hum of the machine. She felt like she was in high school again. Surely, this wasn't the first time he'd helped with her bike.

"How long have you been back?" He shouted above her handlebars.

"Just got in this weekend," she answered, bending down as though to help. "I can do that," she added, reaching for the cap as he moved on to the back tire.

When he was done, Zack stood and clapped his hands together. "All set. You want a lift home?"

She shook her head. "No, thanks. I'm trying to get my miles in." *Miles!?* Since when did she go from zero activity to *getting her miles in*? She closed her eyes a moment too long and smiled up at him, a thin, tight-lipped smile of mortification. How could Zack Durbin be having this effect on Becky? How? She gave him up for greener pastures. For *Andrew*. Useless Andrew who took her virtue and gave her Theo in return. It was a great deal, no doubt. In fact, she'd do it over again times infinity just to have her sweet son.

But now, looking in the face of the very thing (the very *person*) she'd sacrificed for a foolish, college romance . . . well, it made her feel all twisty and weird inside. Disappointed and guilty. Guilty for not calling Zack when she could have. Guilty for thinking that she should have called him when her priority was Theo. And, at the time, Andrew.

Too many men. That was Becky's problem.

Then, he hit her with it. A total bombshell. Out of left field. Despite her decidedly bedraggled appearance and the fact that while he grew hotter she grew more matronly.

"Well, maybe we can have coffee sometime."

But that wasn't the most shocking event of the morning. Oh, no. The most shocking event was her own reply.

"You're welcome to come up to the farm right now, if you want.

Chapter 8

Amazingly, he *did* want to. But she had already turned down a ride. So now she either had to bike home while he drove there *or* (and just as embarrassingly) she'd have to retract her "miles" comment and accept the ride. A ride with Zack wouldn't be so bad in and of itself if she was freshly showered with new make-up and a decent outfit.

Too late. As soon as she started to waffle, he hefted her bike into the bed of his truck. "You don't need the exercise anyway," he commanded with a wink.

Becky's heart rate quickened.

The ride to the farm was silent. She thought it could be quiet rage. Seething silence. After all, Zack had every reason to hate her.

But if he hated her, then why was he being so nice? And why was he joining her for an eleven o'clock coffee in the dead of summer? And why the wink?

"Wow, it looks exactly the same," he remarked as they pulled up to the farm. Then he added. "In a good way."

Becky smiled.

Comfort took the place of feverish anxiety the moment they made it to the porch. Zack had visited a few times during their relationship those many years ago. Memaw loved him. So did her mom. And of course Zack was close friends with Ben anyway. He was practically family.

Grandbern had come around, too.

But those facts did nothing to soften Memaw's reaction when she, still dressed in her Sunday best, opened the screen door in time for Zack to step up behind Becky.

"Is that Zack Durbin?" Wonder and maybe a tinge of fear lifted Memaw's hooded eyes halfway up her forehead. Becky reached an arm through the open door in case her grandmother fainted, though that would be quite the overreaction.

Zack dipped his chin and answered, "Yes, ma'am."

Becky supposed it was her turn to smooth out the details of such an unexpected visit, but then—what *were* the details? Even she herself was unsure why she invited him. Unsure why he *came*. Unsure what they would do.

The teenager in her took over and she began to slide past Memaw as she rushed out a half-baked response. "Zack's here for coffee, but I think we'll go with the sweet tea. Be right back!"

Excitement bubbled over top of the anxiety in Becky's stomach. She knew Memaw well enough to know the woman could outtalk a hairdresser. And company on a Sunday? Surely there was no greater gift from God himself. They'd be just fine.

Becky had no choice. She had to sneak a shower. Shave. Make-up. The whole bit. But spending even half an hour primping would be unreasonable. No time for second guessing. Becky knew she missed a chance those eighteen years ago. Maybe she didn't have a chance anymore. Maybe she didn't want one. But a woman north of forty was surer footed than a girl of nineteen.

She was going for it.

***

Memaw and Zack's conversation flowed from the porch into the living room. Becky took a moment to check on Grandbern before heading out to join them. He was snoring softly in his recliner. The television set projecting another ball game. Sweaty iced tea sat half-drunk on the metal T.V. tray by his elbow. His oxygen tank pulsed more slowly, but with each mini burst Becky felt a whole minute tick away.

She pecked her grandfather on the cheek and whispered that she loved him before smoothing her sundress (*too much?*) and stepping onto the porch in her bare feet.

Becky could hear that Memaw was in the middle of one of her stories, but as soon as the screen door slapped shut, so too did Memaw's mouth.

Well, *actually* her mouth and Zack's wagged open a bit.

"Hi." It came out on a breath. Zack stood from the porch swing, nearly falling back into it when it swung out and in, knocking the back of his knees.

No one laughed.

Memaw excused herself, and Becky began to take the old woman's seat in her plastic Adirondack chair, but Zack waved his hand toward the swing.

She agreed, scooping the back of the dress beneath her as she eased down onto the rickety wooden slats. His weight pulled her toward him a bit so she scooted away. Only slightly.

The question burned on her tongue but asking would release a fire. So she kept her mouth closed and stared ahead at the green yard and out into the woods beyond.

Zack cleared his throat. "So what's up with your last name?"

She turned to him, her eyebrows furrowed. "What do you mean?"

"You corrected me. You always used to correct me. But today you corrected me then corrected yourself. Becky Linden-Spaur. But you haven't lost the Spaur yet. Are you trying to lose him, too?"

Blood crawled up her neck and bloomed into her cheeks. He had gumption, after all. And some to spare. She could feel that he was staring straight ahead, too, though. Not daring to press her with a hard gaze or guilt her with a cold stare. Should she answer? Should she ignore him? Should she cry out for Memaw to come back?

No. Becky was an adult, as trying as that was. She swallowed and sniffed, giving him one more chance to change the conversation. He didn't, though. So she answered him in as even a tone as she could muster. "I already did."

A quick glance in Zack's direction confirmed that he had no real reaction. It hurt. Maybe he did need to leave. Maybe this was a dumb idea. Maybe she mistook a blink for a wink earlier at the corner store.

The swing shifted beneath her and back they went. She looked at Zack, who was now smiling sadly as he lifted his feet. She did the same, locking her knees and staring at them. After three swings, he abruptly planted his feet. Her whole body slid forward across the slats until she put her feet down, too. It was a silly dance. Zack had no reply, but she'd promised herself she was going to follow through on whatever this reunion was.

"Zack," she began. He turned his face to her, the smile still there. She continued. "I'm sorry."

"For what?" He answered.

She blinked at him and turned to face him now. His expression was soft and open. He wasn't mad. She'd misread him. He was confused. Maybe even sad.

Sometimes, sad was way worse than mad.

Her jaw muscles clenched and unclenched. This could go two ways. Like most paths in her life, Becky chose the harder. "I'm sorry for moving to Arizona." She cringed. It didn't come out quite like she meant. Of course.

Zack frowned and shook his head. "Why would you apologize for that? You moved to Arizona like I moved to Notre Dame. Neither of us had any right to keep the other from an education."

Becky smiled. He had told himself the same thing she'd told herself. That their parting was mutual. He wanted bigger and better and she wanted to show him she could let go.

If only she could.

Becky considered apologizing for the rest. For finding new "love." For . . . Theo. But she would never apologize for Theo.

"You could have called, you know," he said.

Becky agreed. She'd already been through this with Maggie. But then she realized something. It fell out of her mouth. The start of a fight. Or the start of a resolution. "So could you, you know."

They locked eyes and he shook his head. "I mean . . . after."

She knew what he meant. It was one thing for them to get trapped in the first few weeks of school. The adjustments were brutal for both. Maybe more so for Zack, who was under the thumb of a Catholic school, too. Becky's freedom was the problem, maybe.

"I would admit it was a mistake, but you know I can't do that, Zack."

"Becky, I would never ask you to regret having your son. Don't be ridiculous." His eyes pled with hers and a hardness shaped his face.

"Yeah, well." Sure, her defenses were still up. She wasn't being ridiculous. So many people felt disappointed in Becky. Her entire family had only met Theo once, when he traveled to Chicago with his junior high school's historical society. Memaw and Grandbern made the road trip. Becky couldn't join. She had to work. Stay ahead of bills. Pay for the darn trip, of course.

It was a strained, emotional affair, according to her mother, who had even flown in for the occasion. Her mother, who now had a little money thanks to her new boyfriend/husband. Her mother, who hadn't come to Theo's birth or his first birthday or fifth or tenth. Hadn't bothered to drive down to Arizona from California to heal things. Help.

Becky glanced down at her pale yellow dress. Her tanned legs, freshly shaven. She lifted a hand to her hair and brought the long strands forward over her shoulder, breathing in the clean, floral notes from Memaw's Herbal Essences. Becky's favorite. "I have to pack," she said at last.

"Pack for what? You just got here."

She shook her head and pressed a hand to her temple. "I mean *un*pack. I'm tired, I guess."

He stood and stuffed his hands into their pockets. "Let's go for a walk."

It was just like him to defy her.

And she loved it.

***

Pleased not to have wasted good makeup, she agreed.

As they walked down the long driveway and toward Main Street, which was less of a main street and more of a green-framed country road, he kept his hands in his pockets and his lips together.

Without him there, she might enjoy the stroll. She clasped her hands behind her back and took a deep breath as they began the descent toward Little Flock Cemetery, the mound of stones on the corner.

"You okay?" he asked after she'd exhaled and clapped her hands back in front of herself.

She smiled and nodded her head. "My lungs aren't used to the thicker air, yet."

Together, they slowed when they came to the corner where the cemetery protruded from the fork. "Where to?" He waved across down Main Street and then left, deeper into the back hills of Hickory Grove.

Her eye caught the schoolhouse in the distance off past Main Street. She pointed to it. "Remember?" Wet air clung to her lungs. Sweat broke out in the hollow of her lower back.

Zack stared past her then nodded carefully. "Sure do." Becky watched him for a beat. His strong jaw much the same as when they were teenagers. The skin around his eyes tanned and rougher. He cleared his throat and stepped to the left and up toward the back hills, away from the school. "Let's go this way."

Becky's heart sank, but she followed. Once they'd passed the cemetery, she threw one more look over her shoulder toward the little house in the distance.

Silence and time wove together until they were on a trail. The same one that would lead back to her family's farm. Disappointment swelled inside her but she forced it down, changing her mind about keeping her mouth shut. "Zack, hang on." She came to a full stop. Poison ivy snaked past her left ankle. Tall oak trees towered over them like eavesdropping giants.

He turned and slipped his hands from their pockets. His Adam's apple bobbed, and he jutted his chin. A shoulder shrug. She took it as her cue.

"Why did you come over to the farm today if you don't have anything to say?"

He swayed back. "What? Are you kidding, Becky? I'm waiting for *you* to say something."

She frowned. "I already apologized, what more do you want."

Zack shook his head. "I don't need another apology. I need you to open back up, girl. Stop acting like you're nervous. Or scared. Like a wounded doe."

She rubbed the back of her hand over the dew that formed at her hairline then dropped her arms, palms facing up. "I'm not scared," Becky replied, feeling itchy now. If he was going to accuse her of being weak, then she would move right on out of Hickory Grove. Forever. She could not live there suffocating with guilt. She eyed the poison ivy and scooted right half a step.

A smirk came across Zack's face, propelling her back to their last date. The one before each would take the long drive to college. His drive, of course, would be padded by the company of his father. An SUV packed to the brim with carefully selected dorm room accessories. Meanwhile, Becky loaded up Grandbern's rusty 1980s pick-up and without little more than a parting hug, sailed off into the sunset like some sort of tragic renegade. She'd cried the whole drive to Tucson, three days' worth of tears interrupted only by rest-stop naps.

Their last date wasn't at the schoolhouse. It was in the bed of that pick-up truck before she'd hugged her family goodbye. They were eating cherries and spitting the pits into the woods behind the farm. They agreed to make no big to-do about the leaving. She'd call. He'd call. A tentative winter visit was in the works. When she glanced at him sidelong and asked, with caution, that he remain faithful to her, he smirked.

Just like now.

Becky moved closer to him. One step. Two. "I'm not nervous, either."

He dropped his head and matched her movement. One step. Two.

Then, under the blanket of trees and heat, Zack Durbin wrapped an arm around Becky's waist and tugged her into him. Her breath hitched as her cheek hit his shoulder. He took her head in his hand and whispered down, "*Maybe I am.*"

Chapter 9

They'd walked back to the farm, hand-in-hand. She thought about her life. How she regretted some parts but not most. Her regrets were the usual suspects. Not calling home more often. Not scraping together money to join Theo on his school trip.

But did she regret how things went with Zack?

Once they'd arrived back, Zack begged off. He had to get back home. He was working on his roof. That explained his tanned face.

He had acted like he might kiss her on the front porch, but Grandbern had woken up to a start and called out for another sweet tea. When Memaw didn't answer inside, Becky had to leave Zack.

But something lingered in the air after he'd driven off. And for the first time since she'd returned to the farm, her stomach wasn't cramping with anxiety. It was fluttering with butterflies.

Becky returned to unpacking and realized that all she had learned during their time together that morning was how much she missed Zack. How she felt about him. How those feelings never went away in spite of time and space and *life*.

She didn't learn who he was, however. Who he'd become. What time had made him. What space did to him. Where life took him. She kicked herself for keeping those questions in her heart like hostages.

The next day, she again took her bike to town. This time, sailing down hills only to push it right back up until she arrived at the old diner where her mom had worked.

Grandbern had been asleep in the recliner when she'd left. Dressed up in his plaid button-down and jeans, with a sweaty iced tea melting on the T.V. tray, the oxygen machine breathing life in and out of him.

Memaw had to change the bedding but refused Becky's offer of help. Typically, Becky would not have even offered. She would have simply taken over. That morning, however, she felt an urgent need to get out. Between the car trip and the stale farmhouse air, she was under threat of an early case of cabin fever.

She told Memaw she intended to inquire about a job. Her meager checking account needed a boost if she was to help pay bills and see to it that Memaw and Grandbern had enough to enjoy their golden years and what little time they had left. Besides, she'd promised Theo she would make sure he had the basics covered.

And, waitressing was one of various jobs she'd held over the years. That, bank telling, secretarial work, and administrative work. Becoming a waitress at Mally's would be like following in her mom's steps. Maybe not very glorious, but certainly comfortable.

A tinny bell clanged above Becky's head as she pushed the door open and stepped back in time. She wondered if Leroy was still cooking back there. Maybe Ruby would come around to snap, "Take a seat anywhere, hun!"

No such luck.

All new employees. None who might recognize the little girl who read books in the back room. It made Becky wonder how new people found their way to a frumpy place like Hickory Grove. Where had they come from? Where exactly did they think they were going?

Then again, could it be Hickory Grove that was changing? Growing, after all? Had she been wrong to assume it was the same as it always had been?

After noting the paper sign that read "Please Seat Your Self," she plucked a menu from the plastic tray and slid into the nearest booth. Same items; new names. Whoever was running the joint these days definitely wasn't Mally. His locally named dishes were now generic. Mally's Mighty Burgers were just hamburgers. Breakfast All Day had been reduced to a footnote: no breakfast served past eleven.

The harried waitress whisked over to her, pen hovering above a notebook. Mally wouldn't approve of that either. He always made his staff memorize. No matter what.

"What can I get?" She asked, tapping a foot on the peeling linoleum floor.

Becky set the menu on the table and smiled up. Curiosity got the best of her. "Is Mally around?"

The waitress snapped her gum. "Mmhmm, nope. He passed a few years back. Kathy Matthew's in charge these days. Her 'n' Bill."

Though she never knew Mally well, a full-blown sadness filled Becky. She shook her head and asked for a coffee and pancakes. "Oh, and . . ." she added, "Are you all hiring?" Her hometown twang made itself known and the woman softened, at last.

"I'll ask Bill." A warm smile replaced impatience, and she pulled the menu away, returning behind the counter and calling to someone in the back.

Becky pulled out her phone. Maggie had texted, asking if she wanted to come over for breakfast. *Too late now*, she began to respond but the waitress was back with a piece of paper. "Here you go. Fill this out and bring in a copy of your proof of residence, driver's license, and three letters of recommendation. Bill says he'll keep your application on hand for when an opening pops up. 'Kay?"

"Thanks," Becky answered, deflated. What small-town diner required letters of reference? Certainly she was overqualified.

And proof of residence? Maybe this Bill fellow knew Grandbern and Memaw and would shrug off all the lame requirements. Maybe these strangers weren't the outsiders.

Maybe Becky was.

She picked up her phone and asked if Maggie could join her there, at the diner.

No, came Maggie's answer. Little ones here, remember. ;)

Becky told her she'd be over after a quick bite and coffee. They could catch up and relax.

"Slow the freak down," Maggie shouted over squabbling children. Becky sank into the chair farthest away from the commotion.

Brief introductions had meant nothing to Maggie's heathens, but Becky already adored them. From a distance, she adored them even more. Maggie turned back to cereal boxes, pouring and sliding them across the kitchen table before pulling her own chair closer to Becky. "You had a *date*!?"

"No, no." Becky corrected. "We went for a walk. It was the most awkward hour of my life. Or two hours, I guess. From the corner store to the farm and all the way back. He was cold then hot then cold then hot. I guess I was, too, maybe. I don't know."

"I'm here to tell you that man never sold his heart off. He came back to Hickory Grove for one reason and one reason alone, Beck."

Becky raised an eyebrow and sipped on a mug of Maggie's weak, grainy coffee. "You mean his father's business, right? To take it over?"

Maggie shook her head in slow, loping swoops. "If that were true, then dontcha think he'd be *taking over his father's business*?"

"You said the other day he might be!" Becky accused, pointing a finger at her friend.

"Yeah, well. I put out my sensors."

"You mean feelers?"

"Whatever." Maggie laughed. Becky, too. "You might think I was the one pining for you all these years, but I got myself a new gang, girl."

Becky's face dropped and she feigned shock. "You traitor!"

They laughed again and Maggie explained. "Being a mom in Hickory Grove is the same thing as being in high school in Hickory Grove. Eat or be eaten. Anyway, we aren't close enough to share a washer at the laundromat, but we're close enough to gossip ruthlessly. And anyway, my mom's friend, Shelby, is in love with Zack, so I knew she'd have all the deets. And she did."

"Maggie, you can't bring your friends into this, especially if one of them likes Zack!"

"Oh, please. She knows she doesn't stand a chance. It's just fun. Shelby is married, anyway." Maggie waved a hand, effectively dismissing the matter. Becky belted out a laugh. Hickory Grove was much the same as ever.

"Okay, so spill, Mags. What does Married Shelby know?"

"For starters, she knows that he definitely works for the school. It's not a part-time gig. So those times I saw him around were legit. Secondly, she knows his dad is livid that Zack never joined him at the 'practice.'" Maggie raked her long, fake nails into the air to form quotes. Her kids pushed away from the table and zoomed out of the kitchen, their cereal bowl remains sloshing in their wake.

Becky watched them run off and thought about Theo. He'd been a rambunctious kid. A hellion as a toddler, in fact. The terrible twos had lasted well into kindergarten. Those early years were hard. But she made it. And now here she was, back in Indiana, just miles south of him. Notre Dame. It felt a little funny. Together but apart.

"Okay, so he works for the school. Are we positive he ended up studying law, then?" Becky asked.

Maggie set down her mug and delivered a measured reply. "No. We are only sure of one thing." She paused, dramatically. Becky's eyebrows pinched together in worry. A smile dancing on Maggie's mouth and brightened her eyes. "He knew you were coming home and was asking around about you."

Becky's jaw about hit the table. "How do you even know this? How do your *friends* know this?" She felt her heart thud in her chest and her pulse tingled at her wrists and throbbed in her neck. She swallowed and stared hard at her silly best friend who was more likely to tease her than be honest for once.

"It's true. It's all Ben. Have you seriously not spoken to your brother, Beck?"

Becky shook her head then stopped. "Well, yeah. I texted him that I would be back this weekend. For a while. Maybe for good. He replied that they would come down and visit soon. That was it."

"Well," Maggie replied. "That's the answer, then."

"What do you mean?" Becky asked.

"Ben's wife's sister is one of my new friends. She is a transplant from New Albany. Apparently you are fodder for the rumor mill which is exactly why I gained traction with this little mommy clique. So when I texted the group, they were all up in arms, citing a specific text exchange. I don't recall the fine details, but I know that Shelby was the most . . . excited. Which was all I needed to know to find out the truth."

"And what, exactly, is the truth?" Becky pressed.

Maggie breathed in and breathed out. A child screamed in the background, stilling the bottle blonde only for a moment before she answered Becky. "They're fine," she said as she flicked her hand behind her before going on. "The truth is, Becky. Zack has been waiting for you to come home ever since you left."

Becky sighed like a girl. *If only*, she thought. "Actually, I'll tell you the truth, Mags," she began to answer. "The *truth* is I might not stick around, after all." Sure, Becky's plan was to stay in Hickory Grove for some time. But the disappointing job search at the diner was a bad start. And if this weirdness with Zack didn't take a true shape, she couldn't handle it. That hug was the best and worst romantic moment of her life, but did he realize that?

"Bull honkey," Maggie cried. "You're back for good. I know you, Rebecca Linden. We just have to get you settled."

Becky smiled. "Well I'm looking for a job, so if you could put your 'sensors' out for something, that'd be a start."

"What kind of gig?" Maggie asked.

She sighed. Good question. She hadn't put much thought into it. "I did a little bit of everything in Tucson. I volunteered at the library, of course. I tried to apply at the diner, but they aren't hiring. So, I'm open-minded, I guess."

Maggie nodded, her face serious. "Are you on a time crunch?"

"The sooner the better, you know. My bills aren't going to wait around."

"My friend Brenda was between jobs recently, and she went to a life coach to help get some clarity," Maggie answered. Becky rolled her eyes but listened. "The coach said that you should always start with your dream job and go from there. It gives you focus."

"My dream job was to be a librarian. But I don't have my degree. So what comes next that actually pays? Because volunteering to host the Book Babes Book Club on Thursday afternoons definitely won't put money in the bank."

Maggie laughed. "Okay, yeah. Sure. Books. I get it. What about working at the school? Maybe you could read to kids who are failing the third grade or something?" This time, Becky laughed and shook her head.

"Let me be clear. I need money to cover insurance, groceries, and Theo's bare necessities." Thankfully, Theo earned a hefty scholarship, qualified for financial aid, and promised to work part time. She said she'd cover everything else. Or close to it. She had to make good. And then there was her plan to help Memaw with the mortgage or electric bill. Or any emergencies.

"What about getting a job in New Albany? They have bookstores, at least. It's a shame Hickory Grove kids can't walk down Main Street and buy their own ding-dang books. No wonder our test scores are mud." Maggie began to launch into a tirade about her own educational philosophy, but Becky slapped her hand down onto the faux wood table. Maggie jumped. "What is it!?"

"You're right, Maggie!" Becky shouted, grabbing her friend's hands.

"Of course, I'm right," Maggie answered, smirking. Her smirk turned down. "About what?"

Becky eyed her mischievously. "Hickory Grove needs a bookshop."

Chapter 10

Becky and Zack hadn't spoken in a couple days. But they *had* texted.

They shared a couple borderline flirty emojis and generally kept their message sessions brief and superficial. She'd comment on nice weather. He'd tell her about how he was building a pergola for his dad.

Each time she began to ask what he did for work, she changed her mind and deleted the words. What they did for a living was an in-person conversation. She wanted to save those things for when they were back together.

He might have agreed, since he never asked her anything deeper than how she'd slept. Waking up to a sweet text made her feel like a schoolgirl again. And the words and questions that went unspoken provided her with hope. Something to look forward to. An unplanned date, perhaps.

While she waited for Zack to make a move, Becky watched muted baseball games with Grandbern in between helping Memaw with housekeeping and cooking. In her spare time (of which she had plenty), she alternated between job hunting and researching how to start a business.

Maggie, Grandbern, and Memaw all loved the idea of a bookshop. When she talked to Theo (finally), he asked if Hickory Grove was big enough. Surprised by both his insight and unusual pessimism, she felt a little discouraged.

"Why not go down to the Chamber of Commerce, darlin'," Memaw suggested. "They might help."

Becky nodded her head as she wiped down the kitchen table and returned the rag to a soapy sinkful of water. "That's true. They can help with the basics. But how would I even start to acquire books? Will it be a used store? New?"

Grandbern shuffled with his walker into the kitchen, resting every few feet.

Memaw propped her hands on her hips. "Where's your tank."

"I don't need it," the old man waved her off, cranky as a canker sore. "I wanted to come join the conversation for once, if that's all right by you two?" His eyes fell on the sheet of freshly baked cookies Memaw intended to drop off at the church for a fundraiser the next day. Knowingly, she lifted the batch from the counter in front of poor Grandbern and whisked it away to the adjacent counter, scooping and sliding the cookies into cloudy, old Tupperware. Over her shoulder, she answered. "We'd love your input on Becky's bookshop."

"What bookshop?" he asked.

Becky smiled. "I might like to open a little store in town. I don't have a location, though. Memaw, I bet I could just go hunting for used books and sell them a little higher. Maybe I could sell your cookies, too. And put out a bulletin asking for wholesale goods from whomever in town wants to sell their wares. Or maybe sell stuff on consignment or whatever."

"All great ideas. I think you ought to visit that shop up in New Albany to get started. Learn the ropes. Maybe you get a part-time job there," Memaw suggested. "While you learn about the business."

Grandbern began to cough. A loud, wheezing affair. The old woman crossed to him and took his elbow, redirecting him back to the recliner, where his oxygen tank awaited. Becky followed catching a commercial on the television set. An online tutoring program for students of all ages. *Get individualized support in math, science, reading, writing . . . anything you need!* The voiceover declared.

She thought for a moment about Maggie's dissatisfaction with the school, wondering if it was Maggie's lazy parenting or if there was a real need in Hickory Grove.

"Grandbern, what was school like when you were a kid?" Becky asked. Memaw draped an afghan across her husband's lap and kissed him on the forehead, rubbing it in like she used to, when she wore lipstick. *Even farmers can wear lipstick*, she would say, when she slathered on the red.

Memaw eased down into the rocking chair that sat adjacent to the recliner, and Becky curled up into a spot in the crook of the sofa nearest Grandbern's chair.

The oxygen tank exhaled a few times before Grandbern worked his mouth into an answer. "Well, we had just one teacher for all of us. There were the little kids on up to eighth graders. Once you was done with eighth grade you moved over to the high school."

Memaw interrupted. "That's where we met, you know, Rebecca." She gave Becky a pointed look, and Becky smiled. She did know, but she always loved to hear the story.

Memaw's family was from New Albany but moved down for the cheaper land. Both of her grandparents claimed it was love at first sight. In Mrs. Sanderson's second hour history class. *And the rest was history*, Grandbern used to joke when Memaw would recount the first moment their eyes locked. He hadn't used that joke in years.

"My Aunt Edna was my first teacher there that I can remember, and she was sweet as pie. Then we had that awful woman. *What was her name?* That's when my best friend, Harold, dropped out, come to think of it." He went on, and Becky cherished every note, every detail.

She cut in to ask, "Do you know who owns the schoolhouse these days? I can't recall. Is it privately owned now? No one is taking care of it. I have a right mind to go over there and do some cleaning, but I'm going to need more than furniture polish and bleach, I'm afraid."

Grandbern reclined a bit and shook his head, his eyes growing heavy. "We can discuss it more later. I'm pretty tired now." Memaw reached over to push his tank a bit closer so it wouldn't topple as he laid back to rest.

"Becky," she half-whispered across the room. "What an idea!"

"What do you mean?" Becky replied, uncurling her legs to stand up.

Memaw stood first, motioning her into the kitchen. When they got there, the old woman raised her voice in a crescendo. "You could set up your shop in the old schoolhouse!"

Becky felt her body tremble. Her skin prickled in goosebumps and her breath hitched.

Memaw was right. It was brilliant.

The old schoolhouse could use a reno. Waxed floors. Shiplap across the crumbling interior. The scene grew in her mind.

She could rehab the student desks into product displays and bookshelves. The teacher's desk could be a check-out counter. Just might need a lift and a good polish. She may even need to bring in a contractor to rehab the foundation and walls. It was in pretty bad shape. But it wasn't a total loss. Not yet.

The smell of warm, pine-scented candles filled her nostrils, now. Books organized by author and genre. The Dewey Decimal system.

She could have a little corner cafe against the back wall, where Memaw might stock cookies and serve sweet tea. Becky could make bookmarks and other little crafts to add to each customer's brown-paper bag.

Becky blinked and her slow-growing smile froze then fell into a frown.

Sometimes, a good idea—even a great one—fell short of practicality. Owning a bookshop was a dream. Hickory Grove needed one, too. The children sure did.

But Becky was flat broke. To make money, sometimes you really did need to have it. Sadly, she shook her head. "I wish you'd never had suggested that Memaw."

The old woman frowned, her mouth pulling deep into her neck. "What's the matter with it?" she pressed.

Becky answered, lamely. "It's perfect. It's just perfect. But I can't afford to buy the schoolhouse or fix it up just the same as I can't afford to go buy a bunch of books to sell."

Memaw dropped her chin and looked over into the living room to assure herself Grandbern was out like a light. Then, she turned to the junk drawer that sat collecting everything from scissors to screws to batteries and pushed stuff around for a moment. At last, she held up a wrinkled envelope. Across the front had been written *STOP! DO NOT THROW AWAY!! PRIVATE!! 911!*

Like so many things that Memaw had begun to do, the warning made less sense than she probably realized, but Becky loved her all the more for it. She looked at Memaw, her eyebrows furrowed. "What?"

Memaw slowly unpeeled the flap and pulled out a thick stack of bills. Becky watched as her grandmother's wrinkled hands flipped through the money and then patted it on the counter, at last pushing it across to Becky with a meaningful expression painted on her wan face. "It's yours, Becky. I was going to wait and add it to the will, but I didn't want Ben to make off with it."

Becky's eyes grew wide at both the gesture and the green pile in front of her. Mostly, at the fact that Memaw wanted to cheat Ben out of something. She shook her head and held up her palm, but Memaw again pushed the pile forward then took Becky's hand and covered the bills with it, pressing it down with surprising strength. "This is not a choice. You'll take the money, or . . . or I'll just burn it. I don't want another word about it until I know you bought that dang old building."

A nervous laugh escaped Becky's mouth at her grandmother's singular swear. But Memaw was gone. She'd swept her old body out of the kitchen and down the hall to scrub a bathroom or something.

Becky peeled the money apart, quickly realizing it was a hodgepodge of ones, fives, tens, and twenties.

It amounted to two thousand, four-hundred, and thirty-eight dollars. Memaw's life savings, no doubt. Becky found herself more stuck than ever. Now she *had* to buy the schoolhouse and make something of it.

She had no choice.

***

A visit to the Chamber of Commerce was indeed the right first step. There, she got a packet on small-business ownership and information on being a local business owner in the greater Kentuckiana area. But the best nugget of information she had was *who owned the schoolhouse.*

The answer was surprisingly simple. It had never changed hands. Hickory Grove Unified School District owned the schoolhouse.

***

A musty smell filled the carpeted waiting area at the district office. Becky didn't mind it. She pressed her purse into her body and strode toward a vaguely familiar, bored-looking woman behind a wood-paneled desk.

"Hi, my name is Rebecca Linden. I'm here to inquire about the little one-room schoolhouse out off of Overlook Lane?" She kicked herself for her tone. She sounded weak. The district office receptionist surely thought so as she continued typing slowly on her computer for several moments before turning her attention up to Becky.

Becky cleared her throat and started over. "You might remember my family. The Lindens up off Main Street. We've all gone to school here. Well, I'm here to learn more about the one-room schoolhouse."

The woman blinked. "I have no idea what you're talking about, hun." She laced her fingers and sat them in front of herself next to an ancient, boxy desktop computer. Becky changed tactics.

"Is the superintendent available?"

"Mr. Engelhard is on lunch right now. Can I take a message?"

"No, I'll wait." Becky turned and took a seat before the useless woman could reply. No magazines existed in the seating area, so Becky pulled her phone out and returned to her research. Currently, she was googling how many books a new bookshop ought to carry. It was a starting point, at least.

In a separate browser window of her phone's tiny screen, she had a job search up. In order to carry out the schoolhouse plan, she needed something to pay for it. And if it weren't for Memaw's secret cash advance, she might have given up as soon as Memaw had suggested it.

But now the family legacy was resting with her. She had no choice.

Five, ten, then twenty minutes ticked by while the secretary alternated between making personal phone calls, filing her nails, and printing pages only to swear under her breath and fiddle with the printer.

Maybe she'd get fired and Becky could have that job. She silently asked God to forgive her for the cruel thought then returned to swiping in her little phone. She thought her stress would vanish when she moved back home.

Instead, it seemed to quadruple. But in her heart, Becky knew that she had to have the schoolhouse. It was as much a part of the fabric of her life as Theo. It was one of those things that made her who she was. Having the pressure from Memaw was just the kick she needed to start the second half of her life. The best half, maybe.

Just as she gave up on scrolling through local job postings (none *truly* local) and clicked to tuck her phone away, a familiar voice addressed her. "Becky? What are you doing here?"

Standing above her, in a smart-fitting suit and matching tie, was Zack Durbin.

Chapter 11

Becky followed him down a dated hallway lined in photographs of Hickory Grove High School football players. By the time they turned into an office at the back of the hallway, the photos had aged considerably. Becky wanted to stop and stare at them. The goofy early uniforms with their puffy pants and plain jerseys.

"Come on in here." Zack waved into a generic space with a conference table framed by rolling office chairs. He must have read the question in her eyes as he pulled out a chair for her to sit in. "Not my office." He gave her a moment to settle before offering her a coffee or water.

Becky shook her head. "Is this the superintendent's office?" Confused, she tried to remember if she'd given the secretary any indication of what she wanted to talk about with the superintendent.

"No, no. I'm just here for a few hours today. I don't technically work out of the D.O. I'm kind of like an independent contractor for the district. On retainer. I have several contracts throughout the county. I have to say, though, Hickory Grove Unified is my favorite. I love to know I'm giving back to my community." He was babbling. Nervous, even. She smiled.

"So, you handle business for the superintendent? You're not a teacher? I was hoping to talk to Mr. Engelhard about something."

"Oh, right. He's at lunch. Maybe I can help. Maybe not, but I wanted to say hi at the very least." Zack scratched the back of his head then met her eyes with a shy smile. She thought back to their tight squeeze. How she wished she had the gumption to turn it into a kiss and undo all the years of heartache that grew between them. Like a maxed-out balloon. Ready to pop. She bit down on her lip.

"Hi," she answered, her eyes sliding away only to dart back at him. She could have sworn he rolled an inch closer to her. A lump crawled up into her throat, making it hard to share the reason she came here.

Zack seemed to sense this and leaned back a bit. "Are you applying?"

She blinked. "For what?"

"For a teaching position. They have a few last-minute openings," he answered, his eyes on fire.

Hope flashed through her chest. She'd never given a lot of thought to the career that everyone else saw her in. It would have been logical. Books every day. Sharing her love of reading with a captive audience. "I don't even have a degree," Becky admitted, looking down at her hands.

"Oh." Zack shifted uncomfortably.

"That's okay. I am here about a job, in a way," she began, twisting to look at the door. She'd rehearsed what she would say to this strange, powerful superintendent. Wasting her spiel on Zack might be back luck.

Though no conversation with Zack would be a waste. Of that she was certain.

When Becky turned back, Zack lifted his hand and covered hers. "Becky," he started. Her pulse quickened, and her neck grew hot. "I'm sorry."

She forced herself to breathe, shaking her head in confusion as she kept her eyes locked on his.

Zack cleared his throat. "The other day I never gave you my apology. And I couldn't do it in texts. I was about to ask if you'd like to get together again. So I could say it. I guess you beat me to the punch." A smile replaced his fretful face and squeezed her hand before sliding his own away to his space on the table.

Becky let out a small sigh and beamed back at him. They could move on now. Get back to where they'd left off, maybe.

"So what do you do for the school? I never knew if you'd become a lawyer like your dad or a school teacher like you'd dreamed of." Possibilities began to surface in Becky's head. If he was close to the powers that be, he might be able to help her buy the schoolhouse. Or negotiate a rental agreement, ideally, since she had no down payment and no source of income. The impracticality of her dream didn't escape her. Embarrassment began to replace excitement.

"I'm sort of both. Well, technically a lawyer. I represent Hickory Grove Unified which is why I don't have an office here. I pop in about once a week and attend school board meetings. Why are *you* here, Becky?"

A vibration in her purse cut off the delicious sound of her name on his lips. She ignored the buzzing. "Well, it's a long shot," Becky began, fumbling with her words. She began to pick at her nails. Her cell phone kept vibrating so she kicked her purse gently to reposition it. "I'm trying to get some information about the schoolhouse." Another glance back toward the door revealed no sight of this supposed superintendent. A new round of buzzing crawled up the base of her chair and she reached for her purse, blindly slipping her hand inside to mute whoever was spamming her. Had to be Maggie. Then Becky's mind leapt to Theo.

No. He was fine. Surely.

"Oh? The schoolhouse. What is your interest?" Zack's tone shifted subtly. More businesslike. Cooler.

Becky swallowed. Again, her phone buzzed. "I'm so sorry, would you excuse me to check this? It must be important."

Zack nodded and rolled back a little to give her some degree of space.

Again, Becky pulled her phone out of her purse, this time hoping to catch whoever was calling rather than silence them. The name MEMAW lit up the screen. She frowned at Zack, accepted the call, stood, and turned her back.

Her voice low, Becky answered. "Memaw? Is everything okay?"

The old woman's voice was surprisingly calm. Grandbern was rushed to the hospital. Life support. Clots. Very serious. Last rites. Come now.

She froze, willing herself not to cry. Not to react. Not here. Not now. Grandbern had to be fine. It was an overreaction. The doctors were wrong. Memaw misheard. It was fine. *He* was fine

Becky nodded, forcing herself to breathe and keep it together and listen intently without turning around and falling apart. Once Memaw had finished the report, her voice cracked and fell away. The call ended.

"I can't breathe," Becky whispered.

"Becky? What's wrong? Is everything okay?" Zack was beside her in a flash, his hand supporting her elbow. The lump in Becky's throat gave way to a sob. There was no possible way she could just recount everything she'd heard. "Is it Grandbern?"

Gratitude filled her and the sob broke loose into hysterics. The only thing that saved this moment was Zack. What if the superintendent had to witness this? In her moment of anguish, she was thankful to be with someone who didn't need an explanation.

Someone who knew her. Knew everything about her. Even if they'd been apart for ages.

***

Zack drove her to the hospital. Becky typically suffered from serious car sickness when she was a passenger. But car sickness couldn't compete with heart sickness, so she indulged in examining the landscape as he sped from the district office the fifteen miles into Greenway, the next small town over.

Familiar storefronts and homes whirred past. Speed limit signs and red lights did little to slow Zack's racing truck. He ran at least two, which wasn't too hard since no traffic impeded their path.

Maybe she was living in a movie, where everything fell into place for traumas like a very sick grandpa. In real life, you had to sit in traffic for half an hour while white-coated doctors and blue-frocked nurses scuttled around your loved one, calling out desperate commands and stealthily avoiding tragedy.

Zack knew better than to say anything. He let her wilt in the seat, her phone clutched in her grip. What if she had answered after the first vibration? Would it have made a difference?

Grandbern was a farmer. He was supposed to live until he was a one-hundred-year-old raisin. He was supposed to live until everyone was happy for him to slip six feet under like his ancestors before him.

They crossed into Greenway and a memory formed in Becky's mind.

Zack showed up with carnations requesting a meeting with Becky Linden's parents.

Ben had greeted him at the door, confused that his friend had shown up to see his sister. "We don't have a dad, and our mom ain't home," he'd told Zack.

Becky appeared behind him, confused and entranced by the surprise appearance of the adorable boy from math class. The one who'd complimented the schoolhouse. The new kid.

"Well, who can I see about taking your sister out, then?" Zack asked Ben.

Ben puffed his chest and turned around to glare at Becky. "You can talk to me," he answered, his voice dipping into a lower octave.

"You can talk to me, young man," Grandbern's garbled voice cut across the living room as the old man ambled from the kitchen toward the front door. "What's your business here?"

Becky shrank away in humiliation, tucking away near the hallway as Ben dashed off upstairs to his room.

"Hi, um, Mr. Linden?" Zack squeaked from the threshold.

"Yes, I'm Bernard Linden. Rebecca's grandfather."

Zack cleared his throat and dropped the flowers. "Well, sir. I'd like to find out if I could take your granddaughter on a date."

"Well, son, you'll have to ask her, then, won't ya?"

Becky's eyes grew wide at the unexpected turn of events. Grandbern turned and waved her over, and she obeyed, nearing the door in her frumpy sweatpants. "Hi, Zack," she whispered, her eyes downcast.

"Hi, Becky. Wanna go out?" Zack asked, his voice shifting into its normal tone.

"Sure," she answered, darting a glance at Grandbern.

Memaw overheard the conversation and joined in, wiping her hands across her apron. "What's goin' on?" she asked from behind Grandbern.

"This young man is here to ask Rebecca on her first date," he declared.

Becky winced at the word "first," and looked up to catch Zack's reaction. He didn't bat an eye. Instead, he held Memaw's gaze and nodded severely.

"Ma'am. I'm here to see if Becky would like to join me for a date. Here you go." Awkwardly, he shoved the carnations at Memaw and then stepped back into position. Becky stifled a giggle.

"Becky?" Memaw looked at her granddaughter with fire in her eyes. "Are you goin' or ain't ya?"

Becky nodded vigorously. "I'll just go change," she answered before darting off to find something respectable to wear.

Grandbern and Memaw must have left Zack to wait in the living room, because Becky could overhear their voices moments later from their bedroom next door. The walls in the farm house were paper thin, something that was highly bothersome at night when Grandbern snored.

But it was also highly useful when Becky wanted to listen in on her grandparents' conversations.

"I thought you hated lawyers, Bernie Linden," Memaw accused. Becky reddened as she smeared Chapstick across her lips and tugged on a pair of jeans that Maggie had left behind the weekend before.

"Lindens don't hate anyone, Faithy. And especially not someone who shows himself to be a good man."

***

Becky snapped back to present as Zack opened her car door and led her from the emergency room parking lot into the chilly waiting area. The walk back to Grandbern's curtained-off bed was too long and too short all at once.

Zack whispered that he'd wait outside, but Becky grabbed his hand and squeezed, refusing to let go. He squeezed back, following her through the narrow slit into a tight space, where Grandbern lay propped up on a bed.

Oversized tubing pumped air into his chest, which throbbed up and down like a scene from a science fiction horror film. But unlike a movie, doctors and nurses were not racing around the hard-working machinery. They weren't so much as checking his pulse or swapping out I.V.s. Instead, one simply studied a monitor. Meanwhile the doctor stood next to Memaw, speaking in hushed tones.

Becky caught her grandmother's gaze and the women began to weep in tandem, Memaw striding to Becky and whispering into her ear that she loved her.

Until this moment, Becky figured it was dire but not final.

And then the priest walked in.

The question now was whether to wait for Ben and his wife to arrive. Becky's mom was en route to the airport but wouldn't get in until the evening. Should they wait for *her*?

Zack kept mum until Memaw turned to him, a trusted ally in her eyes. "What do you think, hun?" She asked.

He shook his head, wholly uncomfortable. "This is a family decision."

"That answers it, then," she replied. And so they waited.

Memaw. Becky. And Zack.

Ben came, without his wife. Sat for a while in the room until he couldn't handle it and left for the hospital cafeteria.

Then, hours later, Patsy arrived.

The priest, who'd never left, instructed them to form a small circle.

The last rites were emotional. Sobs cut through the Father's blessing. Memories swirled in Becky's mind. Regret. Happy times. Sad times. Memaw swayed on her left. Zack squeezed her hand.

The nurse removed Grandbern's ventilator. His chest collapsed into a sunken hollow beneath a white sheet. The skin on his face transformed quickly from frozen anguish—a man unrecognizable—to calm peace.

Becky couldn't believe her timing.

Then again, it was just like him. Grandbern wouldn't have gone and died if she weren't around.

In that moment, among tears and hugs and helplessness, Becky realized that her grandfather, her hero, had waited for her.

What she didn't realize, was that he wasn't the only one.

Chapter 12

Memaw, much to Becky's surprise, had been well prepared. She and Grandbern had plots in Little Flock Cemetery. She could have had the ceremony earlier in the week, but she had read in her ARRP magazine to give it a few days.

"It's important to allow the grief to settle. Closure starts before the funeral and ends with the last handful of dirt," Memaw said to Patsy on the morning after Grandbern's passing.

"You'll never really have closure," Becky's mom argued back. Ben was at the table tapping away on his phone. Becky stirred sugar into a fresh-brewed pitcher of tea. The older two Linden women were also in the kitchen, Memaw scrubbing the oven (therapy cleaning, she called it) while Patsy sat rummaging through a stack of old mail her parents had saved for her.

"You're thinking of grief, dear," Memaw replied from her uncomfortable position on the floor. Becky rinsed her ladle and set it in the drying rack before bending over and insisting Memaw hand her the scouring pad. She could do that while Memaw worked on oiling the cabinets.

The old woman shook her head and wouldn't give up the pad.

"Memaw, you don't want to pull a muscle this week. You can clean something else. I'll work on this."

Memaw let Becky help her up and continued to answer Patsy. "Funerals give closure. It's the grief that lives on forever. Like a little heart murmur. Never goes away but you only really notice it right after the doctor tells you that you have it. And every other time your breath stops. Or if you have a small pain. You always wonder if it's the murmur or something else. In this case, it will be the murmur." Her voice broke off so she scrubbed a bit harder.

Patsy waved her mother off absently and changed the topic. She wanted to hear all about Theo's trip to college and how he was doing.

Painfully, Becky obliged her. "Maybe we could make a little family drive up there next week or something, Mom? Theo would love to see you. I'd love to see him."

Patsy shook her head. "Oh, honey. I wish I could. Randy has a family reunion in Washington, and I promised him I'd go. Isn't he coming for the funeral?"

"Yes, that's true," she replied softly. She hadn't wanted Theo to come at all. It might be awkward—his happy presence against a depressing backdrop of mourning country folk. But he told her he'd be there, if just for the day.

She finished the oven and began to leave, glancing at Ben on her way out. He looked up. "Where you going, Beck?"

"Outside. Going to walk the woods for a bit. Want to come?"

Ben stood and nodded his head, shoving his phone into his pocket first. "Sure."

Lazily, they walked out onto the front porch and down the stoop.

Bugs buzzed around them as sunlight dried the morning dew.

"You know, Becky, most universities have a family weekend in the fall. You ought to set something up. Get a hotel room for yourself. I'll drive up to see Theo. I bet Memaw will come with me."

Becky's face lifted. She and Ben had never been particularly close. Their different interests coupled with Patsy's distracted affect did little to seal them together in an unbreakable twin bond. But that didn't mean there wasn't a deep love.

"I'd love that," she answered, letting the idea sit between them as they slipped down a little trail Grandbern had cut through the woods years ago.

***

Ben had asked for it. He needed a bike trail, he said. Grandbern told him he'd clear the trees and work on it if Ben helped him.

Everything started out gung-ho. Ben and Grandbern made a good dent into the vast Linden acreage, but after two weekends, Ben had lost interest.

Becky supposed he found a trail somewhere else.

The day after Ben's declaration that he was too busy to help Grandbern anymore, Becky descended from the house, passed by the chicken coop and through Memaw's garden and inspected the trail with careful attention. It was of little use to her. She had the schoolhouse. That's where she and Maggie liked to play. And it was a good spot for Becky to escape to.

However, she hated to see the disappointment in Grandbern's face. His grandson gave up on their joint project. Didn't fulfill an unspoken promise. Let him down. So, that same day, she swallowed her irritation with her brother, stomped back into the house and declared she would help Grandbern finish the trail.

His eyes glowed at her and off they went. Into the woods to get the job done. They changed the plan, shrinking the scope of the project considerably. Now it was a short loop out and back in.

A month later, during which they were only able to work when Becky was out of school and Grandbern was caught up on farm business, they'd finished.

"A perfect strollin' trail," Memaw had confirmed, proud as could be.

"It needs a sign," Becky added, searching the area for a sense of what might best describe it. Grandbern and Memaw agreed and set about a week-long brainstorm. Each night around dinner, they would pitch their ideas as Ben shrank deeper and deeper into a pout.

Patsy would even chime in. "Something fancy! Like Villa de Hickory Grove."

No one liked that one.

"Or maybe something like: The Bridge by Becky, Ben, and Bernie!" Memaw offered, beaming with her own brilliance. The whole table laughed except Becky.

"First of all, it's not a bridge. And second of all, Ben didn't even help," she whined. Ben's eyes watered with shame and anger. Patsy nodded her head in silent agreement with her daughter. Memaw clicked her tongue.

Grandbern shot Becky a stern look. "That ain't true. Ben was the one who had the great idea to begin with. And he did help. He got 'er started. A good start, too. There wouldn't be no trail if it wasn't for Benjamin."

Adolescent embarrassment bloomed red on Ben's face, but he sat as still as he could, eyeing his grandfather with cautious appreciation.

Becky remembered feeling embarrassed, too. She didn't want Ben to be excluded. She also didn't want Grandbern to think of her as a brat.

An idea had popped into her head. "I know! Let's have Ben choose the name of the trail!"

The whole table gasped and oohed over the suggestion. Ben, still embarrassed but less angry, considered it.

***

They stood at the opening to the trail. Becky hadn't been out here since she'd returned. She stepped to the corner of the entrance and pushed back a scraggly branch, revealing the decades-old wooden sign.

"Linden Lane," Ben said aloud, chuckling. "How *original*."

"How perfect, you mean," she answered, smiling back at him. They walked the short loop, catching up. Becky enjoyed hearing about his kids. His job. His busy wife who opted to stay with the children and allow him a private trip for a serious occasion.

Becky considered asking Theo to stay home. Maybe it was better if it were just the trio. Maybe it was no time for a family reunion. Her heart ached with indecision and sadness.

Ben listened as she gave him a boring account of her clichéd life. She wrapped up with a deep sigh.

"You have a lot to be proud of Becky," he replied when she was done. She shook her head and looked at him, strangely. He nodded and continued. "You're a good person. You've done the right things in your life. As right as you could. We didn't have a clear path to success, you know?" He blew out a puff of air. "Mom was always so caught up in her own life. Of course, we had Memaw and Grandbern's undivided attention . . . when they were done working the farm for the day. But no money. I wasn't sure how the heck you were gonna get to college. But you did."

"But I didn't finish," she interjected, lamely.

"You got started, didn't you?" He smirked and she socked him lightly on the arm.

"I guess we're both good at starting things. Maybe not finishing them." She sighed as they emerged at the end of the child-sized trail.

"Are you going to finish your degree? Become a librarian?" he asked.

Becky smiled that he remembered her dream job but then shrugged. "I'm not sure. Maybe one day. Right now I am trying to get settled. Or figure out if it's worth settling here."

"Have you . . . ah . . . talked to Zack?" He averted his eyes and his tone told her he already knew she had.

Becky stopped walking and crossed her arms. "Yeah. I suppose that's another thing I started but didn't finish, huh?"

***

The church service was a crowded affair, as were most funerals in Hickory Grove. Grandbern had always likened Hickory Grove funerals to contentious town council meetings that had been called to address the need for a tax hike. People showed up who otherwise didn't much care. During the two or three funerals they'd attended as children, Grandbern would lean over to Becky and Ben, pointing generally at the mass of darkly dressed people and say, "Do you think these people ever showed up to his birthday supper?" Or "Do you think these here folks was around when she was in the hospital with gallbladder?"

It was just the thing to do, Becky reckoned. Nothing going on this Saturday? Check the paper for a funeral.

Memaw looked as beautiful as she ever had in a black pantsuit with her finest jewelry. Maggie set her hair for the occasion. Patsy helped her apply a bit of lipstick and leant her a pair of dark sunglasses.

Theo had come down, after all. The re-introductions went smoothly enough, and he even opted to ride to the funeral with Ben. Becky liked that. They needed to bond. Theo needed it.

When the women climbed into Patsy's car on the way to the graveyard from the church, Memaw whispered low that she'd just lost her bookend.

"What do you mean?" Patsy asked, assessing herself in her rear-view mirror.

Memaw looked to the backseat at Becky and Maggie, who had asked to ride with them. The girls smiled at Memaw, and she smiled back. A sad smile. But a smile. "I guess you've never been in love, Patsy." Memaw answered, laughing to herself. Becky was happy to see her grandmother in such good spirits. She didn't understand how the woman wasn't a total wreck.

Relishing her moment to play a wise old lady, Memaw explained what she meant. "Your life is a mess of books. Books here, there everywhere. But you have a few books that you love so much you decide, 'I'll put these ones in between those ol' bookends I happen to have. They'll be safe. They won't get lost. Or roughed up. They'll look nice for company.' Well, of course, bookends only ever come in pairs. Sure, you could shove a stack of books against one side of a shelf or maybe a big rock and prop the other end up with that leftover bookend that's been sitting around. But good bookends come in pairs and stay together, doing their job. Working to keep a set of books safe. Bookends don't sit side by side most of the time. But that's a good thing. They are working like a team. Bernie and I were good bookends. We held together a long stack of books. Classics and cheap books alike, actually. I suppose when you're sitting there, as a bookend, for so long, holding in so many books and maybe losing a few over the years, you don't stop and think about the other end. Who's down there holding up the other side? When the man you love dies, you realize, 'Oh. That was the other book end. I forgot. Now I have no one to help me hold all these books together. To sort these memories and these responsibilities and every single thing that makes up a person's life? What is going to happen to all these books between the bookends?" A sob escaped Memaw's mouth and she pressed her hand to her lips.

Becky leaned forward and whispered into her ear. "Memaw, I can help you with the books, you know."

The old woman's face creased up into a smile, and she said, "I was hoping you would, Rebecca."

***

Once they met the priest at the cemetery, Becky glanced around for familiar faces. The crowd had lessened on the ride over. Most people resumed their normal activities, heading to lunch or back home to catch a ball game. Grandbern would have. He'd have said there was no point in watching them bury a man. Too morbid for his taste. He preferred to ignore the fact that our bodies never truly left the earth. That they were still here. Dead. Beneath us. Becky shook the thought and caught a figure in the distance. She thought she'd seen him at the church but was too distracted with accepting condolences.

Now, as Memaw, Patsy, Theo, and Ben took their positions in front of Grandbern's plot and Maggie found a place directly behind them, Becky wished Zack were up there with her, holding her hand. Being her bookend as they added this tragic title to her shelf.

She swallowed down the tears but they kept coming, through the service to the end, after every visitor had his chance to toss a handful of earth on top of Grandbern.

Some closure. Becky thought.

After, Memaw accepted more hugs and well wishes and Becky slid away, choosing to walk through the headstones. When Maggie called out to her and asked if she was okay, she hollered back that she'd walk home. Maggie simply nodded and rejoined the others as the crowd thinned out.

Becky glanced toward Theo, who was immersed in a conversation with Ben. It warmed her heart. Theo must have felt his mom's stare, because he stopped walking and looked around the hill for her. When their eyes met, he held up a hand in a wave and then mouthed, "Are you okay?" She nodded and shooed him off.

A few strides later, she began to search, too—for Zack.

Maybe it was indecent of her, but they'd spent the intervening days texting further. He continually offered help, but she continually turned him down, preferring space and time to be with her family.

He respected it.

But even Grandbern wouldn't want her to thwart his advances forever. She made a silent promise to accept Zack's next offer, whatever it was. Coffee. Dinner. An exclusive meeting with his boss. She rolled her eyes at her half-baked plan.

Owning the schoolhouse was a joke, really. It was impossible. It would take an act of God, probably.

She began to feel sick and slowly came to a stop at the top of the cemetery hill and stared down over Hickory Grove, her gaze settling on the crooked little building down off Overlook. Maybe she didn't have the deed. But it still felt like *hers*.

"Let's walk over there," came a deep voice behind her. Becky gasped in shock and turned to meet Zack's sad eyes. She wiped at a stubborn tear and nodded, taking his hand as he led her down the backside of the cemetery.

He let her walk in silence until they came to the pasture that would carry them to the schoolhouse. Becky slipped out of her flats and walked barefoot through the grass, carrying her shoes in one hand as her purse flapped against her hip. She glanced up to Zack to catch his expression as they neared the old place. Did he remember? Did this abandoned one-room building live in his heart like it lived in hers?

"Do you remember our last time here?" His question made her heart race and her face grow hot.

She smiled. "Of course." They stopped just outside the front door. She began to put her shoes back on and move forward, inside.

"Becky, wait. Don't go in."

"Why?" she asked, confusion and bemusement filling her face.

"It's not safe. I don't want you to get tetanus or something." A laugh escaped his mouth but his eyes were serious.

She appreciated his concern but waved him off and strode around the side to the back entrance that'd she'd used a week earlier. "Come on, silly." She coaxed him.

Inside the room with Zack felt different. Gone were the little girl memories of her time with Maggie. In their place came clandestine evenings with her high school boyfriend. Their meetings always bordered on scandal, which now made Becky feel a little wanton. Uneasy.

But, alive. Very alive.

Becky watched Zack circle the room, studying each corner like it was his job. She broke the silence. "I never told you why I was at the school district office."

He stopped at the wood-burning stove and looked up, meeting her gaze steadily. "Why were you?"

"I want to buy this place," she said, holding her arms out then adding, "I *have* to buy this place."

He didn't answer. She felt herself grow hot and amended her statement somewhat. "Or lease it. Rent it from the school, maybe?"

When he still didn't say anything, she began to sputter out her rationale, but he strode over to her and slipped his hands around her waist. Then, in a way that felt unromantic, he hugged her. Hard.

A fresh set of tears welled in her eyes as he pulled back, confused. Did he think it was a great idea? A terrible one? "Zack, what's wrong?"

He shook his head and bit down on his lip. "Can we talk about it over dinner some time?"

Chapter 13

Of course, she'd said yes. Maybe he'd been uneasy about asking her on a date after Grandbern's funeral. Maybe that had accounted for the awkward hug and rushed goodbye.

None of it had bothered her. For once, Becky felt like she was heading in the right direction in her life.

But once she'd returned home to Memaw and her mom and Ben and Theo, a weirdness settled over them. Her mom had to return to California and Ben to New Albany. Theo couldn't miss another day of classes.

For some reason, their brief visit felt nearly as sad as Grandbern's death. A part of Becky wondered if this was how it would be for the Linden family. Reunions only during funerals. Never weddings or babies. Just death. They would show up to pay the respects that were otherwise inconvenient.

She couldn't begrudge her mom or her brother their priorities, however. And certainly not sweet Theo, who'd gone above and beyond, for an eighteen-year-old.

Becky, herself, never pushed hard enough to come back for any reason at all. Not even ancient Aunt Edna's passing back in 2000. Relationships were two-way roads. Even crummy relationships. Maybe especially crummy relationships.

Once a few days had passed and the reality of Grandbern's death felt more normal and a modicum of boredom swept through the empty farmhouse, Becky turned her focus to Zack, replying to his texts more quickly and with more fervor. They danced around the idea of a date, neither one committing quite yet. But neither one offering any real excuse to delay. Becky figured her reason was grief. Maybe Zack's was his busy job.

Almost obsessively, she reflected back on their youthful relationship and fast-forwarded through the fantasy, wondering what if, what if, what if.

Like a teenager, she began to envision being with him again. Every waking moment turned to Zack. His face: older. More handsome. His body: fuller. Sexier.

One morning at breakfast, as Becky was absently stirring sugar into her coffee and building up the courage to finally dial Zack's number rather than reply to his most recent text—*Good morning, beautiful*—Memaw intruded. "How's it going with the schoolhouse?"

"Hm?" Becky answered, irritation crawling up her spine.

"You went to see about it and never followed through," the older woman pointed out.

Becky balked. Any tip-toeing around the recent events had evaporated in the last couple days. The two women quickly fell back into their old habits of tinkering around the house and making light conversation—avoiding the hard stuff, unsure what the next morning would bring.

Becky had halted her job search, but only temporarily. She'd learned Grandbern had left a small inheritance to her, Ben, and Patsy. The day after Ben and their mom had left, Patsy called Becky and made a deal: if she was willing to stay on at the farm and look over Memaw, Becky could have the little bit that Grandbern had given her.

It wasn't much. And it was money that came from a guilty heart. Blood money, in a way. But untethered to anything else, Becky easily agreed, wondering when she'd see the check and telling herself she'd set aside her money woes for another few days. Memaw's two-thousand dollars lie dormant in Becky's underwear drawer. Maybe paired with that, Grandbern's gift would draw her closer to a down payment. Or a first month's rent.

In the meantime, it felt good to sit on the porch and read Memaw's plentiful stash of Harlequins. Becky would suck up all the leisure activities she could.

Now, she shook her head. "I haven't gone back to the district yet, obviously. You know that." Worry pulled on Becky's heart. Sure, she had a little money. And she had Zack as a connection (despite the fact that he never did respond to her idea).

But a few Internet searches concerned her. Owning a business was expensive. The upfront costs would require she get a loan. But Becky's credit was average, at best, and then what? She had no collateral. She eyed her grandmother, who popped a slice of bread in the toaster oven and pulled a dish of hand-churned butter from the fridge before returning Becky's stare.

"You don't want the schoolhouse, Rebecca? You'd rather spend the next twenty years working a cash register or weavin' between cafe tables only to come home to rub your aching feet? Listen, girl. I may not have been a wild success in my time. I may have little to show for decades of hard work. But it was all my own. *Our* own." She slashed a finger toward a framed photo of Grandbern that stood sentinel on the china cabinet. "If you respect your granddad and me, then you will march yourself right back to that school district and start living the life *you* want to live."

One minute later, as she paced the front porch, Becky called Zack.

"Zack Durbin, you're taking me to dinner."

***

She had exactly eight hours until he was picking her up. When Memaw laid down the law, she knew the first order of business was a date. With the man she'd never stopped loving.

And even though he would be an easy "in," Becky had no desire to pull him into her business scheme. The two matters were entirely separate.

So, after they made their plans, she began to make phone calls.

First up, was the superintendent's office. There was no way on God's green earth she'd be able to step another foot in his office. Surely she'd incur flashbacks to the moment when she received the worst news of her life. And, anyway, Becky wasn't the type to sit in a plastic chair and wait around for a man who seemed to be on lunch break all day.

His secretary informed her that he'd return her call when he was available. Becky informed the secretary that she'd follow up at three in the afternoon if she hadn't heard back.

But she did hear back. At exactly 2:45 P.M.

"Ms. Linden?" Superintendent Engelhard's voice was softer than she'd expected. Affable. Like he was about to apologize. Though, he didn't. "Thank you for reaching out to me. How can I help you?"

Becky cleared her throat and folded her last pair of underwear, smoothing the stack on her bed and striding to the door. She moved onto the front porch and launched into her rehearsed spiel, starting with the emotional account of her recently deceased grandfather who'd attended the school and ending with her intentions of renovating and reviving the property into Hickory Grove's first-ever historical bookshop. She'd give the school a steep discount, too.

"This all sounds wonderful, Ms. Linden. I'm going to redirect you to another person who will better answer these questions. You see, none of these sorts of decisions are up to me. It's the school board and trustees who determine what we do with school property." He chuckled. "Well, ma'am. Technically, it's good folk like you. Taxpayers, of course. Who vote in the school board members who then vote on decisions. Here, let me give you the phone number of the president of the school board. He'll be happy to answer your questions."

Deflated but hopeful, Becky took the unfamiliar name with the unfamiliar area code and bid Mr. Engelhard a good afternoon.

The president didn't answer his cell, so Becky left a message and pushed aside all of her business plans so that she could focus on getting ready for Zack.

"You are stunning."

Zack stood on the porch, a bouquet of roses gripped like a trophy in his hand. Becky smiled and went to him, pecking him on the cheek and catching a whiff of his aftershave. He smelled the same way he did in high school. Clean and fragrant but masculine. He handed her the roses and offered to fill a vase. She waved him off. "Memaw could be a florist. Let her. She'll tell me where you got these and how much you paid, too. So it's a win-win." Becky winked.

"She'll never guess," he replied, smiling broadly. "I picked them myself from my front yard.

Becky's mouth fell. "You have roses in your front yard? What, are you still living at home?"

He shook his head, still grinning. "Nope. Just enjoying the finer things in life, like gardening. I'd love for you to come by and see. Maybe later, huh?"

She eyed him. "Maybe."

He drove her all the way to the riverboat. Becky was genuinely impressed. And genuinely nervous. She'd never dined on the riverboat. It was the most expensive restaurant in George County. Spanning a quarter of the way out onto the Ohio River, River's Maiden didn't quite feel like a boat or a barge at all. More like a floating palace.

There was only one option: seafood. Becky winced with each crack of the crab leg.

Zack laughed, tucking and re-tucking his napkin into his button-down shirt. "This is why I didn't wear a tie," he joked.

"I wouldn't have gotten in your truck if you were wearing a tie," she answered between bites of succulent, buttery crab meat.

"Sure you would. You still love me, Becky Linden. I know you do." His face glowed as he said the words and Becky wondered why she didn't call him the day she arrived in Tucson. Or the next day after that. Or the next. She wondered why she ever left Indiana at all.

Something nudged her foot, giving her a small start. She playfully glared at Zack while he took a sip of his wine then scooted his chair around the table a little. She frowned, then sipped her own glass.

Something brushed her thigh and she nearly jerked. Speechless and woozy with excitement, she dropped her hand under the heavy tablecloth, finding his hand in the space between their chairs. His fingers laced hers and he leaned toward her, puckering his lips like they were an old married couple who kissed every day. Like it was no big deal. Like they weren't about to have what amounted to a *first kiss*.

Becky swayed into him, and her mouth met his.

Minutes later they were spilling out of the restaurant and onto the dock, where a set of benches leaned up against the railing. Zack pulled her onto his lap, kissing her neck and running his hand up her back. "I've been waiting for you forever," he whispered through her wild tendrils in the cool breeze of the evening.

Becky wanted to freeze in that moment. She wanted to live there. Breathing in Zack and the river and the sounds and smells of the restaurant. Life there, with him, was perfect.

"Let's just sit here for a while," she whispered back. He pulled away and nodded, his eyes shining above the reflection of the water.

She moved her face closer to his and kissed him again, slowly, lazily. Their lips parted, and they opened their eyes at the same time. "Are you really staying in town?" he asked.

"Yes," she answered, moving back to kiss him again. "Of course."

"For how long?"

She opened her eyes and stared into his. He wasn't quite as affected by the wine as she. His eyes were clear, searching. "For how long?" He asked again.

"Forever, I hope."

Zack smiled and framed her face with his hands then pulled her in for a final kiss before he stood, took her hand, and walked her back to the truck. "Still want to see my garden?" he asked.

She yawned and nodded. There was no way she'd stay over at his place, but she definitely wanted to see it. And she definitely didn't want to say goodbye.

On the drive over, their fingers danced circles on each other's palms. When he turned down Main Street toward Rosewood Lane, he broke the happy quiet. "Are you still looking for a job, or do you think you'll just stay on at the farm?"

She knew Zack. She knew *he* knew *her*. Or thought he did. He figured that in order for her to stay in town and *get a place of her own*, she'd need a job. But Zack wasn't poor and never had been. He figured she could live at the farm and not work.

"I have to get a job," she corrected before sucking in a breath and revealing the full extent of her plan. "That's why I'm really hoping to get something worked out with the schoolhouse. I want to turn it into a bookshop. I might tutor on the weekends to help with bringing in more income. Though, I'll still have to work nights at the diner or something, if they ever have an opening. But the schoolhouse is my dream." She looked at him, excited to see his reaction.

"You sure a bookshop would do well in Hickory Grove?"

Becky's grip loosened on his hand and she began to pull it away. He turned onto Rosewood and glanced at her. "Hey, now. I just mean, it's a small town. Any business would be rough. I might know a place looking for extra help."

She studied him through the dim light of the cab. He kept his own gaze ahead.

Becky felt herself grow tense. "All I ever wanted to do was work around books, Zack. You know that. I never got to; I don't have a degree. I mean, I love the schoolhouse. It's part of my past. My family. Memaw and Grandbern think I could do something with it. I . . ." Did she really need to explain herself? And to *Zack* of all people?

He put the truck in park at the end of a long driveway. Becky squinted through the dark toward his house but could make little of it.

She kept going. "I talked to Mr. Engelhard earlier today. He gave me the school board president's phone number. I think there might be a chance." She hugged her purse to herself. "Zack, say something."

"Becky," he began. She wondered why he wasn't pulling in. Why were they stopping here? What was happening? Zack shifted in his seat then turned to face her, the truck engine purring beneath them. "Becky, we're tearing it down. The schoolhouse, I mean. We're tearing it down."

Chapter 14

"Becky, wait, please."

She jumped out of his truck and began to walk home, pretending to ignore the fact that it was nearly pitch black outside. Her phone was almost dead. Using its flashlight would surely kill the battery.

What if she tripped and fell? Broke her ankle and had to limp home? Or what if a bear accosted her? What if she took a wrong turn in the darkness and got lost in the woods?

She kept walking.

"Beck!" Zack shouted after her. "Come back. I'll drive you home, jeez!" She turned to face him.

"Why didn't you tell me?" she demanded, crossing her arms and squinting through the night.

He stopped, just feet away. She could sense him more than she could see him, but her eyes were adjusting now.

"How could I? Memaw called you right after you said you had a question about the schoolhouse. Remember?"

"You could have told me on the phone. Or at the schoolhouse after the funeral. Or at dinner tonight. You had every chance."

"I didn't realize it was that big of a deal to you, Beck." His hand went to the back of his head and he blew out a sigh.

She made a promise to her grandparents. And now that one was dead, so she couldn't very well go tell him that the promise was off. When someone on the other end of a promise dies, you are a true dirt bag if you break the promise.

And anyway, Memaw had a point. Becky was in her forties. Did she really want to start over at the diner? It might be one thing if Mally was still there calling out orders and shooing kids away from the deep fryer. But things had changed in Hickory Grove. "It's a huge deal to me. Maybe not to you. You aren't from Hickory Grove," she spat, desperate to spin on her heel and stomp away. Fear kept her in place.

"I have roots here, too," Zack answered her, his voice hardening.

She dropped her hands. Exasperated. "What?"

"My dad's family is from Hickory Grove. Why do you think we moved back here?"

"What are you even talking about?" As far as she knew, Zack and his dad moved to town—alone—the summer before high school. They were outsiders. No connections.

"I don't want to get into it," he went on. "Do you want a ride home? Or not?"

Becky considered her options. "A ride," she answered, stepping toward him. He turned and walked to the truck where he opened her door and offered a hand to help her inside. She ignored the gesture and settled back into the passenger seat. Her stomach hurt. A headache was forming in her left temple.

Zack climbed in next to her and turned the ignition but didn't move the truck. "I'm sorry, Becky. I made the suggestion to the school board before you were even back in town. It's been slated for a month now. I don't know why Mr. Engelhard didn't say as much. I guess he avoids confrontation. I don't know."

Slowly, Becky turned in her seat. Her purse now gripped in her fingers, her chest hollow. "*You* made the suggestion? Why *you*?" Her brain shuffled through recent memories, landing finally on the wooden log he'd carved. Their initials. It's disappearance. Like it never mattered. Like the whole schoolhouse never mattered to anyone.

Hickory Grove's past.

Becky Linden's future.

About to disintegrate and churn into the sands of time.

Zack met her stare, the glow of the dash reddening his face. "The school had me conduct a safety audit with the head of groundskeeping and the head of maintenance. We inspected every property that belongs to H.G.U.S.D. We all agreed. The schoolhouse is not safe. It has to go."

"So what? No one even goes there, Zack. Who cares if it isn't safe?" Maybe she could still buy it. Maybe there was still time. She saved that idea for a later point in the discussion. A last resort. After all, she didn't have Grandbern's money yet. Would two thousand dollars do anything to sway the school?

"The schoolhouse is an attractive nuisance, Beck. It's just a matter of time before kids or vagrants make their way inside for a camp-out and the whole thing crumbles in on them. Look, I'm sorry. Really." His eyes pled with her, but all she could think about was Grandbern and his distrust of lawyers.

Liable to sue you for just lookin' at 'em the wrong way.

Becky sank back into her seat and crossed her arms over her chest, nodding for him to drive. What would Grandbern say? Would he tell her she was a fool to trust Zack after all? Would he say Zack was weak . . . his father's son. A sue-happy jerk? Would he tell her it was no big deal? Would he tell her he never trusted Zack, after all?

Becky recalled the second time Grandbern met Zack. It was a dramatically different meeting than the first. Her grandfather had surprised in good ways and bad.

***

Date One was dinner at Mally's.

Date Two was miniature golf in the next town over with Maggie and her boyfriend-of-the-week, Spencer.

By Date Three, Becky was in love.

"Zack's taking me to the drive-in," she'd whispered at dinner. Grandbern was refilling his glass of iced tea at the counter. She prayed he didn't hear. Memaw looked up from her fried pork chop. Becky's mom was at the diner, as usual.

"T.M.I.," Ben snorted, scraping the last few crumbs into his mouth and scooting off the bench to wash his plate and head out.

"What does T.M.I. mean?" Memaw asked, her eyes like lasers on Becky.

A sigh escaped Becky's mouth in time for Grandbern to return to the table. Maybe she should have waited until after he settled into his recliner, when it was just Memaw and Becky left in the kitchen, wiping tables and setting the table for breakfast the next morning.

"I don't know. Something Ben made up probably. Anyway," she went on, clearing her throat and raising her voice. "He's picking me up in fifteen minutes. I've got to get ready." She rose as she said it, half prepared to dash down the hall. Half prepared for her grandparents to stop her in her tracks and tell her NOT ON YOUR LIFE!

Neither happened. Instead, Grandbern asked, "You mean the lawyer's boy again?"

"Yes," Becky answered through clenched teeth. Her grandfather was being stubborn. As usual.

"What movie y'all gon' see?" Memaw cut in, covering Grandbern's hand with hers. A smile curled the edges of her mouth. Becky let out a breath.

"Um. I'm not sure. I think we'll just watch whatever is playing for the double feature." Becky had never been to the drive-in. It sounded old-timey and quaint, like something she would read about in a book with a poodle skirt on the cover. She hadn't quite gotten the lingo down, either. All she knew was that she needed to look amazing. Third dates were important, even in high school. It was the moment of truth. Make-or-break-it. Point of no return. After tonight, they were either going to fizzle or be together forever. After tonight, she would know if she was destined to never be kissed or destined to a life of sweet kisses and cuddles with Zachary Michael Durbin. The pressure was on, to say the least.

Memaw raised her chin slowly and eyed Grandbern, who'd helped himself to a second chop and began gnawing away. The old woman's eyes slid up to Becky, and she gave one definitive nod.

Becky's mouth widened into a grateful smile, and she dashed off to add her makeup and body spray, on loan from Maggie, of course.

Zack picked her up at the front door, this time with daisies in his hand. They were a little wilted, but Becky didn't mind, passing them back to Memaw, who stood behind her. Grandbern twisted in his seat at the recliner then made a big show of locking the footrest into place, hitching his jeans higher on his beer belly (or iced-tea belly, as the case may be), and crossing his arms over his chest.

"Sir, may I take Rebecca to the movies?" Zack squeaked from the threshold.

Grandbern huffed. Becky felt herself start to melt into the floor from embarrassment. She peeked up at Zack, whose Adam's apple bobbed visibly from beneath his jaw.

"It's about time I ask you somethin', young man. What are your intentions with my granddaughter?"

Blood rushed to Becky's face. Where was this inquisition the first night Zack had shown up?

She opened her mouth to call it off. Cancel the date. She could become a nun, because after this whole scene, there was no way Zack was hanging around. Not even for a kiss. But he beat her to the punch.

"I intend to get to know your daughter, Mr. Linden."

Becky's heart sank a little. It was the least romantic answer Zack could have given her grandfather.

But it was the right one.

"Be back by ten. I'm trusting you, Durbin."

***

"Wait," Becky pressed her hand onto the dash. Zack slowed the truck, hesitating before turning onto Main Street and down to the farm. He looked over at her.

"What?"

She lifted her arm and pointed straight ahead. "Let's go, come on."

Zack stared ahead into the yellowed spray of his headlights. Their glow didn't reach the schoolhouse, but he knew exactly where she was pointing. His hesitation didn't last long. "All right, then."

Minutes later she jumped out of the truck, ignoring Zack's half-hearted warnings that she might trip. He gave up soon enough and joined her, his phone with its flashlight app lighting their way around the back of the little building.

"Remember that last time we came here?" she asked, determined to move something in him. Make him see.

Zack reached for her waist, steadying her as she climbed the rotting staircase and pushed her way inside. Becky took out her phone, turned on the flashlight, and propped it on the chalkboard tray. It lit the entire room like an overhead projector.

"Yeah," Zack answered after she'd done a brief lap. "I remember," he answered weakly. "Becky, be careful, really. Can't you see why it has to come down?"

"Well, why can't the school just put a little money into fixing it up? It's not beyond repair," she reasoned.

Zack blew out a sigh. "It'd be a total overhaul. No way will a public school district sink money into a rusty, rotted old relic."

Becky stopped in her tracks. She was at the corner of the metal filing cabinet. His words cut her heart, but he was right. If she were being practical, she could see the schoolhouse was little more than a nuisance. Attractive to her, only, however.

Ignoring his comment, she tugged at the top drawer of the cabinet. It wouldn't budge. She wondered what might still be in there that she'd overlooked as a kid. Maybe old science textbooks that would have bored her back then. Maybe papers. She tugged again. Nothing. Jammed or locked. "I can't believe this place hasn't been tagged or trashed," she said after a deep sigh. Then, her face brightened. "Wait, don't you see? It's so deserted. No one is coming around here. Look, Zack." She waved a hand across cobwebs caught in the light of her phone. Isn't this a good thing? See? No one cares. No one is attracted to this old place. You can just leave it up, right?"

Zack didn't answer, but he took a step forward. The floorboards moaned beneath his feet. Becky dropped her hands to her sides, clapping her outer thighs. Now that he was closer, she could see his face clearly. The fine lines around his eyes.

Her mind flashed to the bills in her underwear drawer. She would still try to buy it. She would. But without Zack's support, she felt one step further away. From Hickory Grove. From a happy future. From the schoolhouse.

He lifted his arm and propped on top of the filing cabinet. It creaked, though, and he pulled away, scratching the back of his head with one hand and shoving the other into his pocket.

Becky stared at him. "What have you been doing all these years, Zack Durbin?" she asked.

A chuckle fell out of his mouth, shifting the tone only just. Anger had melted into disappointment which then morphed into a coolness.

"Workin'," he drawled. Becky had missed the southern twang she'd been raised on. People in Arizona didn't sound like her. Theo didn't even sound like her. But Zack did. He sounded just like her and just like her family. She moved closer to him, her heart softening. Maybe even warming.

"What about your dad? What is he up to? Do you work for him sometimes?" Becky had never asked Zack about his mom. It felt like forbidden territory. She considered asking now.

Zack shook his head. "No interest in working with or for him," he replied.

She cocked her head. "He's retired, right?"

Zack took a step closer. "Obviously, Beck. He's eighty years old. My folks had me when they were older. We aren't close. I don't talk much to him. You should know that."

She frowned. No, Becky didn't know that. She had only met his dad once, ever. At high school graduation. Otherwise, Zack hardly spoke about him. "Well, why? Why don't you talk to him? Why did you come back to Hickory Grove at all if you hate your dad?" She pushed her hands into her pockets, too.

He wiped his forehead with the back of his hand and pushed air through his teeth. "All my dad wanted me to do was to become a lawyer and get out of here." Becky raised her eyebrows.

"You mean your dad didn't even want you to take over his business? So who did?"

"I don't know what he wanted for me. He wanted me to come back here and pretend like everything was always hunky dory. Like I didn't miss out on something in life. And the law practice is shuttered. It just sits there. No one is running it." He waved a hand around. "My dad was born and raised in Hickory Grove, Becky. He never wanted to come back."

"Then why did he?" Her voice was gentle but firm. Everything he said confused her, but she wasn't sure where to start. There was so little she really knew about Zack. Where his mom was. What he was like before he came to Hickory Grove. What he did at Notre Dame. And now, now that he was ripping her dream from her grip, she wondered if she even cared.

"I have no freakin' clue." He lifted both hands to the ceiling and dropped them limply, avoiding her gaze.

She *did* care. "So why do you want to stay here so badly? Why did *you* come back here, Zack?"

"For *you*, Becky. Dammit, isn't that obvious? I came back for you." He raised his voice and took another step closer.

But she shook her head. "Well, if that's true, then save this place, Zack," Becky whispered, her eyes trained on him.

He pivoted and walked away. At the door, Zack turned and met her cold stare. "You don't get it, do you? You just don't get it."

Chapter 15

All but one of Maggie's kids were in school. Memaw said the house needed more noise or else she was going to drown in the hollow silence, so Becky invited Maggie and three-year-old Briar over.

"Are you still coloring hair?" Memaw asked Maggie over the kitchen table. Briar munched contentedly on a plateful of saltines while a bizarre cartoon flashed across Maggie's phone in front of her.

"I'm still coloring *my* hair," Maggie answered, chuckling. "And some friends'. I get by on Travis's paychecks. They cover the basics. I get to stay home. It's a win-win."

Memaw took a sip from her glass and set it down, wiping the condensation up the side and rubbing it off on her lap. "So, in other words, you're with him for his money?"

The three women belted out laughing. Truth be told, no one in town liked Travis. The only good thing about him was his steady paycheck from the auto shop. As Aunt Lorna had put it, before she passed, *Travis sticks his dipstick in every ride in town, but at least he'll check your oil for free.*

The laughter fell away, and Becky stared at her best friend before whispering, "Why are you still with him?"

Her friend frowned and slid her eyes over to Briar. "Baby, take that plate and go watch your toonies on the sofa." Maggie glanced up. "Is that all right, Memaw?" The old woman nodded her head vigorously. Gossip trumped couch crumbs in every household in Hickory Grove.

Once Briar was fully occupied and a good fifteen feet away, Maggie crumpled onto the table. "I'm leaving him. There. I said it." Air wheezed out of her like a deflating balloon.

Becky's first instinct was not to whine or wail or console. And neither was Memaw's. "It's about darn time," Memaw declared, banging her fist on the table.

"When?" Becky asked, skeptical.

"I don't know," Maggie admitted, rubbing her bare face with her hands. Becky hoped she didn't rub too hard. Freckles didn't last forever, and Maggie's had already begun to fade. "But I am."

Silence fell across them. Becky had no patience for Maggie's ongoing misery. No one did, in fact. Even Travis was probably surprised that Maggie stuck around. It was illogical.

"Well, in the meantime, I sure could use some help, girls," Memaw said at last, changing the conversation and pushing slowly up from the table.

Becky and Maggie followed the old woman's laborious movement from the table toward the hall. They stood and began to follow. Maggie told Briar to stay on the couch.

After sharing a knowing glance (Memaw never needed help when they were younger. More often, she was the one to offer it), Becky and Maggie joined Memaw in her bedroom. Spread across the bed in no obvious pattern of order were Grandbern's clothes and personal effects. Stacks of boxes towered in on each other in the space between the bed and dresser.

"Where have you been sleeping, Memaw?" Becky asked, amazed at the mess. How had her grandmother even moved so much all by herself?

"Right there." Memaw pointed to a sliver on the far edge of the bed. Sure enough, Memaw had been sleeping there. Snuggled up against a thick pile of Grandbern's button down shirts, her feet likely tucked under a stack of plaid boxer shorts.

Becky smiled. Her eyes grew wet and she felt a good cry pull at her face, distorting her features and stretching her skin.

"No, Rebecca. None of that here." Memaw's voice was stern. Unrelenting. "We're done with being sad. I need your help, not your pity. Not your sorrow. Chin up, girl."

Becky blinked it away and nodded her head. "You're right. I'm sorry. What can we do?"

Maggie offered a smile and rubbed the small of Becky's back. Memaw propped her hands on her hips and surveyed the mess. "First thing is to unload these boxes of papers and go through every single page. Then we can throw out whatever's useless and file away the important. If we have boxes left, we can put the clothes in them to take to the Saint Vincent de Paul behind Saint Ann's."

"Where did all these boxes come from? What's inside?" Becky asked as she kneeled next to the first one, its corners beginning to grow soft with age.

"Grandbern saved everything from coupons to IRS audits. So who the heck knows?"

Maggie laughed; Becky winced. They were in for a tedious chore.

"Maybe we'll find a million dollars," Maggie wondered aloud, amusement filling her voice.

"Maybe we'll find a mummified rat," Becky answered. Laughter cut through their despair. Briar toddled into the room, tears bubbling in her eyes.

"Oh, not you, too." Maggie held her arms out to the ruddy-faced girl. "What's wrong, baby?"

"I want 'nack!" Briar wailed, accelerating into a full-blown tantrum.

"Sweetie pie, you just ate three saltine packets," Maggie reasoned.

Through chest-heaving sobs, Briar managed to choke out a predictable answer. "I want 'nack NOW!"

Maggie sighed and pushed up from the ground. "Stay here, butter. Mama'll be right back." She left to search for her purse, no doubt packed with sugary sweets and salty delights.

"Here, Briar," Becky offered her hand to the little girl. "Why don't you sit with me and help sort some papers?" If Becky knew one thing, it was that nothing fascinated children more than important documents.

Like magic, Briar's tears dried up and she snatched a thick envelope from Becky's hand.

"Did you open that first?" Memaw asked, her eagle eye honing in on Briar's chubby hands.

"Memaw, it's junk mail."

"Well, how can you know that if you didn't even open it?"

Briar dropped the envelope anyway.

"Memaw, you can always tell, can't you?" Becky answered, moving on to a hanging file that was wedged crossways beneath a mound of similarly unopened envelopes.

A sigh bellowed from Memaw's lips, and she tried to distract herself with a different box. "How was your date with Zack, Rebecca?"

Becky thought about how to reply. She hadn't uttered a word about the night before, choosing instead to think things over. If it hadn't been for Zack's heartbreaking role in the impending schoolhouse demolition, she may have dragged him to the courthouse first thing that morning. She loved Zack with all her heart.

"We had a difference of opinion."

"Over what?" Maggie asked as she passed a rice cake down to Briar, who gave up a weak attempt at shredding a yellowed booklet in favor of grabbing the cake and toddling back to the living room.

She had no intention of breaking Memaw's heart a second time. And hearing about the schoolhouse would do just that. It would crush the old woman like a sack of textbooks. Then again, Memaw wasn't very crushable. She would probably dig out the deed for the farm, pass it over, and push Becky back to the district office.

But Becky could never put the old woman in such a position. Ever.

"What is that?" Becky pointed at the booklet dangling from Maggie's hot pink nails.

Maggie lifted the booklet to her face, squinting through faded lettering and reading as though she had only just learned. "Hickory Grove Grammar School Reunion. Eighth Grade Class of 1943."

"Let me see that!" Becky seized the papers from Maggie, studying the cover carefully. On the front was a grainy, photocopied picture of the schoolhouse beneath the words Maggie could hardly make out. Memaw scooted over to her, dodging loose pages and boxes as she made her way.

Once her grandmother was beside her, looking with interest over Becky's shoulder, she flipped it open. It was less a booklet than a pamphlet. An extra sheet inserted included information about meal options and entertainment. Inside the cover included reservation details for the event. Accommodations at the little inn that, when Becky was growing up, seemed more like a museum than a place of business.

"I remember that," Memaw remarked, pressing a finger to her mouth. "Oh yes. Those darned reunions. They seemed to happen every year, I swear. We couldn't go to that one because you and your brother were born that very evenin'. Bernie was upset about the conflict, I suppose. He wanted to go to each one so badly. I told him he could still go to his silly reunion and visit you two in the morning. After all, your mother was adamant about no male visitors in the delivery room. But Bernie said the future was more important than the past. I never forgot that. It was so out of line with Bernie. He dwelled in the past. Until the end." Memaw rubbed her left eye beneath her glasses then clapped her hands to shake the sadness and edged her way back to her spot.

Becky looked for the name of the person to contact about the event, her vague interest turning to intense curiosity.

She skimmed the details of the dinner and information about the local inn. Finally, her eyes pinned on a phone number and name at the bottom of the page.

Darla Durbin.

Becky's breath hitched. Zack had no aunts or sisters. None that she knew of. She was sure of it. And she *knew* his mom's name. It—it just escaped her for the moment. Plus, what would his mom have to do with the schoolhouse reunion? They weren't even living in Hickory Grove until the nineties. *Right?*

Becky asked Memaw if she could keep the invitation. The old woman nodded absently, moving onto a new pile of papers. "Did you know Darla Durbin?" Becky asked.

Memaw paused. "Why, sure. I knew about Darla Durbin. Younger gal, though not by very much. She was doing the same thing you are, Rebecca." Memaw refused to look up from her paperwork, and Becky got a sense she was hiding something.

"What do you mean?" Becky asked.

"She wanted to renovate the schoolhouse. Turn it into a museum, I think. Hmm . . . I think she went to school there just before it closed down. She was friends with Fern Gale's mama, you know."

Maggie's head shot up at that. Any mention of her kooky neighbor seemed to catch her off guard. Catch everyone off guard. Fern Gale in that run-down Christmas house. So odd. Maggie held her hands up toward Becky. "I ain't goin' next door to ask her about some other museum person, Beck," she huffed. "So don't even ask."

Becky sighed and considered Memaw's information. It was outdated, and Memaw was on the fringe of the Hickory Grove gossip circles. But the woman's name was there, plain as day. Darla Durbin. And she was organizing a reunion in 1978. For an older class. Maybe she didn't even *attend* the schoolhouse at all.

"Memaw, is she related to Zack?" Becky asked.

Again keeping her focus on rumbled paperwork, Memaw just lifted her eyebrows and shook her head before murmuring, "Why, I wouldn't know anything about that."

Becky set the invitation on Memaw's dresser and tried to move on. Her grandmother was getting old. Her memory had begun to grow feeble, too. She could ask her more later. Or maybe pressure Maggie into knocking on Fern Gale's front door.

Then, as though it were an insignificant afterthought, Memaw added, with mischief in her eyes, "Oh, I do remember one other thing about that particular year. About Darla, I mean. She was pregnant around that time."

Chapter 16

Her first instinct was to call Zack. And she did, but he didn't answer.

Her second instinct was to call her mother. After all, how many Hickory Grove women were pregnant the same year?

Well, more than Becky probably realized. After all, Becky graduated in a class of over one hundred.

Her mother did answer. "Can't talk, hun. I'm at an event with Randy. Call ya back."

Becky didn't even get a chance to say hi.

Curiouser and curiouser, she thought, as she sat on her bed that afternoon and idly stared at the yellowing invitation. Staring back at her was Darla Durbin's phone number from 1978. The year she was born. The year Ben was born. The year Zack was born, if a bit later on.

Her mind returned to high school. One of her all-time favorite moments with him.

Their senior year, Becky had finally grown trusting enough of Zack to bring him to the schoolhouse for one of their dates. She'd packed a picnic dinner and a little blanket. It was the dead of winter. They'd freeze, probably, but in her mind lots of cuddling would shake the chill.

Once they'd settled into the room, Zack noticed the stove and declared that it was too cold for his Number One Girl. He dashed out the door and was back within minutes with a throng of kindling tucked under one arm and a thick, heavy log under the other.

She'd teased him at first. "And just how do you plan on starting a fire without any matches? That soggy log will never catch, anyway!"

He'd returned with a dead-serious expression. "A real man can start a fire anywhere with anything. Just you watch." And then, like magic, he frisked together two sticks until a low smoke curled across his little pile which he then dumped into the stove. They observed the embers grew to life, and she opened her mouth to ask about the big, wet log, but he beat her to the punch. "This one isn't for a literal fire. It's for our fire." And like a hero in a cheesy romance, he whipped out his pocket knife and carved their initials into the log. B+Z 4ever. Then, he encircled the inscription with a jagged heart before propping the hefty memorial onto the stove top like a married couple might hang their family crest above the door.

***

Carefully, as though each digit might slip out from beneath the pad of her finger, she dialed Darla's phone number, anxious to learn about this woman. This woman who was as invested in the schoolhouse as she. Maybe even more.

This woman who might be kin to her high school sweetheart. The man she thought loved. The man who decidedly had no interest or investment in the schoolhouse.

Her conversation with Zack flashed through her mind. He'd dropped her at the farm, his final words underscoring their date like a stamp of denial. *The demolition is set. The board signed off on a contract with a cheap outfit from Louisville. Sorry.*

But someone else had tried to save it. And not *that* long ago. The schoolhouse hadn't deteriorated that drastically since the nineties. Had it? Plus, this person who tried to save it was Zack's own relative.

Maybe he didn't even realize it. Maybe she was some long-lost cousin of his dad's. Maybe she'd reunite Zack with his elderly father. Possibilities sprouted in her mind.

"Hello?" came a weary voice on the other end of the phone. Becky relaxed her hand, unaware that she'd been gripping it with all her might.

"Hi," Becky began, her inflection an octave too high. She cleared her throat. "Hi, um. I'm looking for Darla Durbin?"

"Wrong number." *Click.*

Becky grunted. She triple checked that she'd dialed the *right* number. Disappointed that she had, she revisited the invitation. Other than Bernard Linden, no names stood out to her. No other contact information was available.

Becky thought yet again about Zack and the schoolhouse. She thought about what this woman went through in trying to salvage it. Why it would have meant something to her. Then, it clicked.

Zack may not care enough about the schoolhouse for Becky's sake (and if that were true, then screw him). He generally didn't care about Hickory Grove's history. But maybe, just maybe, he would care about his own kin. His blood. Maybe he'd care that he had an aunt or cousin who wanted to save it. Whoever Darla happened to be.

She didn't need Zack to help her find this mystery woman. She needed this mystery woman to help *Zack*.

Becky would have to get crafty, though. So, she did some digging.

Starting with Maggie's next-door neighbor.

***

"I'll stay right here," Maggie whispered as they passed through the knee-high fence and over the cracked cement that led to Fern Gale's house.

The front yard was so overgrown that nothing new seemed to be growing. Just dry, tall grass cluttered in lawn ornaments and some rusty furniture. Heaps of overflowing trash bags spit dry leaves from their mouths.

Becky left Maggie at the foot of the porch steps and ascended, gripping the railing with as little of her skin as possible, so as to avoid overmuch dirt and grime.

Busted Christmas lights glistened up from the expansive porch. A dusty artificial Douglas fir tree leaned into the corner, its decorations cloudy and dull. Becky remembered this place before she'd left town. Fern Gale grew up here. With her mom. She was Fern Monroe, then. One of the most beautiful teenagers in Hickory Grove. Just a few grades above Becky and Zack. Though she didn't attend the public school. Her mom had schooled her at home.

And her house—*this house*—had been one of the most beautiful houses in town. The only reason Maggie and Travis could afford buying the house next door was because it had been a foreclosure. It was a great location, Pine Tree Lane.

What a shame.

Maggie and her family had told her how things had fallen apart. Namely, the Monroe house. Becky knew little more.

As she approached the front door, she considered her options. The screen in the screen door had peeled away. The doorbell jutted out on a wire, bobbing in midair a full inch away from its home inside the wall.

She decided against electrocution and instead pulled the screen away from the wooden door behind it and used an old-fashioned knocker.

When it came to door knockers, one knock was never enough. The residents might not realize someone was, in fact, knocking. And, you really couldn't stop at two. That felt incomplete. Of course, going past three was overkill. Three knocks it was.

Becky turned and looked at Maggie, whose eyes bugged from her face as she chewed on a hangnail.

A shuffling noise pulled Becky's attention back, and she took half a step left, so that she wasn't a sitting duck.

Just in case.

"Can I help you?"

Somehow, Becky recognized her voice. "Fern?"

Standing in the door was a shell of the beauty from twenty years ago. Her blonde hair faded into a murky gray, premature for her age. Formerly bright blue eyes sat dull and sunken beneath overgrown brows. Her face was drawn, and she pulled a threadbare cardigan closer against her body as though she might freeze.

It was ninety degrees out. Maybe hotter.

"Yes. Can I help you?" she said at last, squinting at the sun.

"Fern, maybe you remember me. Becky Linden? I grew up here, too."

The woman shrugged, as though it was too great a favor to try and recall an old classmate.

"Well," Becky pushed ahead. "Maybe you don't remember me. You might remember someone your mom was friends with?" Hope dangled off the end of Becky's question, but Fern's face turned even sourer than it already was.

"What do you want, Becky." It was a statement.

Becky felt herself sway back, but she asked anyway. "I'm sorry. I just—well, do you know where I could find someone named Darla Durbin?"

With that, Fern let out a cold laugh. "Of course I do," she spat. "I know exactly where you can find her. "966 Overlook Lane," Fern said and slammed the door shut. The aluminum frame of the screen door slapped back into place, it's netting drifting back into position for a moment as if to regain a little of its pride.

But the netting slid back down, and Becky turned to face Maggie, mouthing the numbers. Her eyes shone bright, and she didn't care if Fern was little more than a grumpy, middle-aged hag. She got what she needed.

"966 Overlook. Let's go," Becky commanded, grabbing Maggie's arm and dragging her back to the truck.

Once they were settled, Becky jabbed the address into her phone, buzzing with anticipation.

She drove back to Main and cut right toward Overlook. Moments later, her phone pinged that they'd arrived at their destination. She hadn't even turned onto Overlook yet. They were at the corner of Overlook and Main.

In front of Little Flock Cemetery.

Becky's heart sank. "Do you think—?"

Maggie glanced her way. "Fern is a nut. I wouldn't trust anything she says."

"We have to find out, though," Becky reasoned, putting the truck in park.

But Maggie refused to join her, instead accusing Becky of becoming obsessed and claiming things were getting too weird. So Becky drove her home back up the hill, where they'd come from.

Still, she, too, felt a pit growing in her stomach. She didn't want to go alone.

Fortunately, Memaw had nothing to do. Becky dragged her grandmother along for the ride. She needed help, and the best way to navigate a family-filled cemetery was to bring an old-timer. You know. Someone who knew the people there.

But once they arrived, Memaw refused to leave the car. She didn't even reach for her seatbelt. "Too soon," she whispered. Becky sighed, but she didn't push it.

So, she brought along her phone, carefully avoiding the fresh dirt mound of the Linden family plot, and examined every other headstone she could in the thirty minutes Memaw was willing to wait.

By the time she had circled the entire area, save for the Linden family plot, she'd come up empty-handed. She hadn't seen any Durbin headstones. Not even names that sort of looked like Durbin.

Trudging back to her little car where Memaw sat, patiently watching from the passenger seat, she threw a final glance over her shoulder. Grandbern's headstone stared down at her, daring her to go near. Becky looked back at Memaw. Though the glare of the windshield blurred her view of the old woman, she saw Memaw nod at her. A firm nod. A nod that said *get back there and solve this thing, girl.*

Becky turned on her heel, twisting a small circle of grass beneath her shoe before pushing back up the hill and toward Grandbern. She fought the urge to cry, focusing instead on the future. Maybe her grandfather really did think it was more important than the past.

In a few months—maybe even a year—Becky would be able to visit his headstone. Carefully clear away the crumbs of dried flowers and replace them with a fresh bouquet. Maybe she'd even unfold a checkered blanket and lay out a picnic lunch, sitting there on the grassy hill next to Grandbern.

But not now.

Instead, she averted her eyes and rounded the freshly piled dirt to inspect the family plot that lay behind that of the Linden one.

Sure enough, there it was, towering over Grandbern's modest stone was a miniature monument. In darkly engraved lettering: *Durbin*. Becky's eyes grew wide. She had never recalled such a garish plot in Little Flock. But it had always been there. The proof was in the names and dates that spread out from the family stone:

Garold George Durbin: 1919-1994

Elsabeth Ann Durbin: 1923-1995

Becky assumed Garold and Elsabeth were Zack's father's parents. Her eyes flashed across the cemetery toward Memaw, who sat baking in the car.

Becky blew out a sigh and pulled her hair up from her neck, now damp with sweat. Searching for Zack's long-lost relative was a long-lost cause. It definitely wouldn't help her win over the schoolhouse. Becky needed a different plan.

Just as she moved back around the Durbin family stone, her foot fell upon a third grave marker. Becky looked down.

Darla Durbin: 1938-1980

Becky gasped and dropped to the stone. She touched the name, her finger dipping in and out of each letter and along the smooth granite. *Darla Durbin.*

And then, it clicked.

Chapter 17: 1996

They had been dating for over a year, but Becky had never met Zack's dad. He didn't talk about his family life, and Becky didn't ask. As a teenager, a twin, and a poor farm girl, she enjoyed that the spotlight was always on her in their relationship.

But she wasn't entirely self-absorbed. Generally, quite the opposite. She'd soon grown bored of basking in Zack's hugs and kisses and the flowers he always brought her. Eventually, she needed more. She needed to *know* him.

They were just outside the schoolhouse, having a picnic in the grass. A late spring frost had only just melted, making their lunch a chilly, damp affair.

Becky had packed strawberries and peanut butter sandwiches which Zack loved. She loved it, too. It was everything a girl dreamed of sharing with a boy.

After each had their fill, Zack yawned and stretched back onto the blanket, closing his eyes for a moment. Becky watched his long, lean body. He wore jeans that weren't too tight or too baggy. The Hollister logo splashed across his chest. His hair spiked in the right places. He could have been a model, living by the beach in California with an equally blonde, tanned girlfriend.

But he was here, in Hickory Grove, Indiana. At the schoolhouse with her.

"Why did you guys move here?" she asked. She knew little about Zack's life. Most of their conversations had revolved around arranging dates or fantasizing about the future.

She loved that about Zack. He wanted a family. With her, he'd even said. He didn't mind when he caught her doodling his name in her notebooks.

Becky Durbin. Rebecca Marie Durbin. Reba Durbin (she went through a period where she tried to change her nickname, but it never stuck).

"I dunno," he answered. "My dad wanted to come back home, I guess. Be with his own dad before he died."

She scrunched her face. "Back home?"

"Yeah," he replied "My dad grew up here. His parents are from here."

"Oh." It dumbfounded her. As far as Becky knew, Zack and his dad turned up on a whim. His dad got to open his own law practice. They got land on which they could build a beautiful home for a good price. It's why any transplant settled on Hickory Grove. Anyway, she knew mostly everyone in Hickory Grove. But she didn't know the Durbins. Although, the last name always did feel vaguely familiar. Like it had lived there in town. Forever. Just under her nose.

She wiped her hands on a napkin and popped a Tic-Tac before crawling over to him and snuggling up along his torso. Zack twisted toward her slightly, bringing an arm down to pull her into him.

Just as she was about to open her mouth to finally ask what happened to his mom, he cut in. "How come your family never *left*?" Zack asked, his voice at odds with their cuddle.

Becky paused. It was a fair question she supposed. But it came across as a little harsh. Pointed. Bordering on rude. "Why would they leave?" She asked.

"Hickory Grove is so small. Don't you want to see the world? Travel? Have new experiences?"

"Is that why your dad left? To see the world?" She scooted half an inch away and pressed a hand onto his ribcage, now straining to make eye contact.

Becky *had* traveled. Thanks to her treasured stories, she'd toured islands and castles. She'd flown the great blue skies and suffered plane crashes. She'd scaled mountains. Becky had seen the Cliffs of Moher and smelled the streets of New York. That her family couldn't afford to take her to those places didn't matter. Traveling was part of her day-to-day.

A serious conversation was unfolding. Perhaps their first serious conversation. Her body quivered with a chill, but she kept her half-inch distance, gnawing on her lower lip in anticipation.

Zack sniffled, and he lifted his chin. "I already told you." He hadn't. "No you didn't," she replied, her voice even. Cold.

"Work." Now it was his turn to scooch half an inch away. They were laying, awkwardly, a full inch apart. Zack returned his hand behind his head. Only her hair was touching his arm now. And it was inadvertent. And neither one could feel it anyway.

"What about your mom?" There. She said it. Finally.

Maybe this conversation would make them closer. Maybe it would help her decide between Notre Dame and The U of A. Between Zack's first choice (which she couldn't afford) and the school which offered her a full academic scholarship plus housing stipend.

Abruptly, Zack stood and patted wet grass blades from his butt. "I don't want to talk about it."

"Zack," she pleaded. "You can tell me. What, did they get a divorce? Lots of people get divorced. Did she just leave you guys?"

He bolted upright, pulling the blanket beneath his hands and accidentally tugging her hair with them. It hurt, but she bit her lip, shocked by his sudden anger. "Just leave it alone, Becky." His voice was louder, colder.

But she couldn't leave it alone. Maybe a new angle would bring him back to her. "So where were you born? Were you born in Chicago?"

"Becky, just shut up. My dad left because things were hard. He couldn't stay here. Sometimes people can't stay around when things are hard."

She knew exactly what he meant. That Zack was just like her father: the one who thought there was nothing wrong with leaving. The one who also left Hickory Grove. And left behind two kids and their mom. Maybe that's what Zack and his dad did to his mom. They just left her. Somewhere. And so she left, too. It was a whole family of people who couldn't commit. Not to a place. Not each other.

The next day, Becky accepted the offer from the University of Arizona.

And she told herself she wouldn't end up like her mom.

Chapter 18

"Did your mom die?" It was raining. A full-blown, Indiana rain. In the middle of an otherwise hot afternoon. Her hair matted to her forehead as she stood on Zack's front porch.

Zack opened his screen door and stood back. "Get in here. You're soaking wet."

It had only been a day, but she was dying to see him. To talk to him. To touch him. To kid and make-up and start over. But even more, she was dying to know if she was right.

Becky accepted his offer, stomping her wet feet on the welcome mat and moving into the air conditioning. A chill tickled her damp skin.

"Let me get you something," he said, leaving her to drain by the front door. She expected he'd return with a towel. As she waited, Becky's eyes wandered around the house. She'd never been in it. Why hadn't he just moved back with his dad? They could be bachelors together. Zack practically lived like an old man anyway.

A masculine feel collided with hominess to strike the perfect balance. It felt like a lawyer's home, she thought. Books lined a wall where a television ought to be. Becky smiled. In the middle of a wall sat a brick fireplace. From the chimney sprouted a plain mantel. On top of the mantel, more books perched on either side of a wooden block that acted like a centerpiece.

Becky's eyes passed over the rest of the space.

Two recliners faced the book wall at an angle, a round table with a lamp separating them. Beyond was a long dining table covered in papers and files folders. A coffee mug acting like a centerpiece to the mess.

She began to walk toward the wall of books, but Zack's return interrupted her. "Here," he said, offering a neatly folded stack of fabric. Becky turned and accepted it, her eyebrows lifting. "You can use my room to change." He waved a hand behind him, smiling softly.

Becky felt her cheeks grow warm. She opened her mouth to ask the question again.

"Let's talk about it after you get dried up, okay?" he replied before she'd even asked.

A chill shot through her, and she nodded and moved into his bedroom.

It was typically male. A navy comforter cut across his double bed. Wooden dressers emitted smells of aftershave and cologne. Becky resisted the temptation to snoop, instead peeling off her soaked clothes and pulling on Zack's gray t-shirt and sweats. She glanced around, considering what to do with her wet clothes. He had an en suite bathroom, which indicated the house was a relatively new build. She walked in and draped her shirt and jeans over the shower door before dipping back out into the living room. Zack was nowhere to be seen.

"Thank you!" Becky hollered into the empty space.

"No problem!" He called back, his voice floating out from, presumably, the kitchen. "Make yourself at home! Just whipping up some sweet tea!"

Becky took a deep breath in and forced herself to be patient. She walked to the bookshelf.

When they were younger, Zack wasn't much of a reader. At least, not by Becky's standards.

Her eyes combed the wall, catching many non-fiction titles. Few novels. Zack had always dwelled in reality. Never fantasy.

But if that was true, then why didn't he find lawyer work anywhere else? Why come back to Hickory Grove? Why would someone like Zack cling to the past?

It was hard to believe.

She let her fingers trail along thick, hard-bound spines until she came to the chimney. Her eyes flit to the mantel. The wooden block that sat between Mitch Albom books and a few Stephen King titles took shape.

It was a clock. A square, rustic clock. The numbers carved beneath spindly hands. The edges coated in varnish.

Becky had never seen a clock that seemed to be carved directly out of the face of a log. She flipped it over.

On the back, a jagged inscription glowed out. An amateur engraving.

B+Z 4ever

Chapter 19

Becky rubbed the palm of her hand across the wooden carving.

"Oh, jeez. I hope that's not weird," Zack said behind her. She turned to see him standing there, one clinking glass of iced tea in each of his hands.

She shook her head. "No. Well, maybe a little." Her eyes flashed up from it, and met his. A panicky look on his face forced her to laugh.

"Let me explain, at least," he said after his own chuckle. "After they agreed that they'd take down the schoolhouse, I went back there. I was worried. I was worried Memaw or Grandbern would find out and get upset."

Becky shook her head. "They don't get the newspaper. All Memaw reads are romance books. They would have had no idea."

He went on. "Well, I thought I'd better save something from it. When I get there, nothing felt like mine to take. I was nervous. Then I saw our log was still there. I figured, 'Well, it was mine to begin with, but it's still part of this place.' So, I took it. But when I got back here with it, it felt stupid. I felt like a stalker. I thought about just burning it, but I couldn't do that. It was yours, too. So, I tried to make it less weird. I turned it into a clock." He passed her the sweet tea, his eyes downcast.

"Were you really just waiting for me to come home?" she asked, momentarily forgetting the whole reason she came here.

Then again. Maybe there were other questions on her mind. Clearly there were, in fact.

"Becky, I wasn't lying about my feelings for you. Even when I heard about your—" an unnatural pause caught in his throat. "Your wedding. Your son. Even then, I still cared about you. Still do." Becky smiled but trained her eyes on the floor. She thought about Theo and where he fell in her tidy life. Made tidy only because she never took a risk. Never disrupted her little boy's life so that she could have her own.

That same tidy life felt like it had grown into a mess. Sure, she was home. But Grandbern left. She had no job (not that she'd looked very hard). Her one interest was slipping through her fingers. And where did things truly stand with Zack? Love was a good start. Enduring love even better. But what was left for them?

Zack cleared his throat. "I came back to Hickory Grove for a few reasons. And yes, Beck—you were one of them. Or at least, *hope* was one of them. But, truth be told, I couldn't just leave my dad. We may never have been close, but he was all I had. Especially once college came to an end." He shrugged and took a sip.

She drank from her glass, too, then asked, "Zack, your mom. What happened? And why can't you talk about her?"

He frowned and shifted his weight, looking for somewhere to set his tea. Becky perched herself onto one of his sitting chairs. He copied her and took another long, slow sip before rubbing the back of his hand across his mouth. "Darla. Her name was Darla."

"What happened to her?" Becky whispered again, staring right into Zack's eyes.

He frowned. "She died when I was two. Yeah. *Here*, actually. Well, not *here* here," he lifted a hand and gestured about. "New Albany. In a car crash. My folks lived on the outskirts of Hickory Grove, in my grandparents' house. They kept to themselves. Dad worked for the school district as a lawyer. Same job I now have. Mom worked for a museum in New Albany. She delivered me there. She was older. Like forty or so. I think." He paused, taking another drink and rubbing his finger across the condensation. "Dad couldn't handle it. People offering condolences. And his parents were so elderly—if not in age in their ways. He knew he'd have to go to a bigger city. Some place with daycare. Hickory Grove wouldn't have the support system he thought he needed, I guess. It was purely pragmatic. So, as soon as he got things in order, we left. Moved to Chicago where he found the same position in a bigger district. I had a nanny. Someone who wouldn't pry or fret over our tragedy. Someone who wouldn't force my dad to talk about my mom."

"He was heartbroken," Becky interrupted.

Zack nodded. "Very."

"So why did he bring you back later?" she asked.

"His parents. Hickory Grove. Mom. He hated the big city. Lots of reasons. And I was older. I didn't need a nanny or anything. So we came back."

Becky let it rest a moment. It was all so simple. So explainable. She was surprised she'd never realized that the Durbin's were *from* Hickory Grove. But if they lived quietly, and if there was a tragedy, then it made sense. People kept mum. Zack's return come ninth grade still made him the new kid.

Why he hadn't told her any of this before, now seemed clear. He couldn't.

But another question lingered. A question *she* had an answer to. "Did your mom *go* to the schoolhouse?"

"What do you mean?" His sad smile fell away and his eyebrows raised.

"She organized Grandbern's class reunion. I mean, I know she wasn't *in* his class. But Memaw said that Darla Durbin was super involved with the schoolhouse." Becky wasn't sure why she hadn't asked Memaw about Zack's mom before. Apparently, it had been irrelevant to her as a teenager. And it hadn't occurred to her once she returned to town. She wondered if Memaw knew the whole time but kept it a secret. Left it for Zack to tell. Becky's heart swelled at Memaw's nature. Her goodness. "Zack, I think she did. *Go* there, I mean." Becky stated it this time.

Zack shook his head. "There's no way. I mean, didn't the schoolhouse close down, like, in the forties or something? It's so—"

"Old-timey?" Becky finished his sentence with a laugh.

He laughed, too. "Yeah. I can't picture my own mom going to school in a one-room schoolhouse."

"But she did." She met Zack's stare. His laugh lines seemed a tiny bit deeper.

The backdrop of his own home framed Zack's grown-up body. His grown-up face. It was surreal. To be with Zack in private like this. In his home. Seventeen-year-old Becky would have just died to have this moment alone with him. Her eyes fell to his lips before she looked away.

"When Maggie and I were kids, we hung out there a lot," she went on.

Zack nodded. "I know."

She continued, "We'd rummage around, amazed at how the place was so . . . so frozen in time. I took some books I had found."

"You? A thief?" he joked. "That's the very reason we have to tear that place down, Becky." He offered a mischievous grin. "Attractive nuisance, you know." And then, he winked.

She blushed through her own smile but pressed on. "One of the books I took was *Little House in the Big Woods*. Inside the front cover, it had a bunch of names, like a high school history textbook or something. You know, how each student who loans the book has to write his name and year inside the front cover?" Zack nodded. "Anyway, I had forgotten about it until I came across Grandbern's reunion invitation, but Zack," she stalled for effect, rummaging in her satchel at her feet. "Look."

Becky opened the decrepit book as Zack stood up and strode over to her chair where he stood awkwardly until she opened her satchel. Then, Becky flipped to the inside front cover and pressed her finger onto the last name in the wobbly list.

Darla Durbin.

She glanced up to catch his reaction. Color drained from Zack's face and a hand covered his mouth. "That's her," he mumbled. "That's my mom."

Becky frowned. "You said she was forty when she had you?"

"Yes?" he replied, reaching for the book and holding it closer to his face.

"The schoolhouse closed in the fifties. The last class to graduate eighth grade did so in 1952. If your mom was forty in 1978, then she was born in—"

"Nineteen thirty eight," he finished for her.

"That would have made her, what? Fourteen in 1952?" Becky added.

Zack nodded. "She might have been in that last class."

Becky let out a sigh. "Keep the book, Zack," she said. "It's yours." Her chest thrummed with heartache for him.

Even with absentee Patsy for a mother, Becky couldn't imagine never knowing your mother. It would be like living without a home. Without something constant.

No wonder he came back to Hickory Grove, she realized.

"Thanks," Zack whispered, closing the book and staring at Becky. "I'll add it to my collection." A smile returned to his face.

"Collection?" she asked. Becky had never heard about it before. Not when they were kids, at least.

"Yeah, my mom loved to read. Just like you, actually." He moved to a corner of the bookshelf and waved a hand. "These were hers. Her favorites. And others."

Becky stepped up to the shelf and let her eyes pass over the titles. Some classics. Some obscure. Some romances, too, just like Memaw. She pulled one from the neatly organized line-up. *Return to His Arms.* She giggled at the sweeping display of a bare-chested man and long-haired woman on the cover. Zack smiled.

"She loved books more than she loved my dad, I think." He laughed. "That's all I remember about her, actually. Her reading."

"You remember her?" Becky asked, unsure how far to push the conversation. Surprised he was even opening up this much.

"Just her reading. I remember sinking into her lap while she read to me. She'd tickle my back with one hand and hold the book in the other, having me turn the pages. My favorite was *The Wizard of Oz.*" A tear fell from his eye, splatting squarely onto the book. He wiped away the wet spot with the pad of his thumb. Becky swallowed down a sob.

In an effort to distract herself from Zack's pain, Becky scanned the shelf for the book. She didn't see it there, among Darla's collection of greatest hits. Perhaps Zack kept it somewhere safe. Or in his own favorite-books shelf along the other side of the fireplace. A pit formed in her stomach. Why had she come here? To rub something in his face? To guilt him into saving the schoolhouse?

"I better go," she murmured and turned from the wall of books back to her satchel on the ground.

"You can't," he said behind her, his voice as fragile as the feathery cover of the book he gripped in both hands. Becky opened her mouth to apologize, to tell him to forget about the schoolhouse. It was no big deal. He had other wounds to tend to. He didn't need to tend to hers, too.

"No, I really should. I'm—"

"You can't go, Becky." His voice evened out and she met his gaze. Amusement took the place of grief and he smiled. "You're wearing my clothes, after all."

Her body relaxed and she let him pull her into his arms. She let him bury his face in her neck as she inhaled his aftershave and marveled at how he smelled just the same as he always had. He smelled like a boyfriend. *Her* boyfriend.

"Zack," she whispered into his shirt. "I missed you."

Gently, he pushed her away and studied her face. "I missed you, too," he answered, chuckling.

"And, I'm sorry. You know. I really am," she went on, ready to rehash everything all over again. But he shook his head.

"You can't be sorry for going to college. I'm not, Becky. We both made our decisions then. And it worked out, right? I mean, I got my degree," he continued. Becky's face fell into a frown. "And you got Theo."

It was all he needed to say. Becky never needed validation. She didn't need anyone to tell her that she was right to stay in Tucson and raise Theo. That she was right to quit school and give up her priceless scholarship. That she was right in every choice she made.

But now Zack was saying exactly that. Theo was worth far more than a degree, of course. But it felt good. "Thank you. Thank you for saying that. I regret the years we lost," she waved her hand between them. "But I could never regret my son. So, Zack. Thank you."

He dipped his head to hers and lifted a hand beneath her chin, pulling it up to meet his mouth in a warm, slow kiss. It knocked her back by nearly twenty years. To everywhere they had kissed. The front seat of Zack's pick-up truck. The backseat of Maggie's car. The parking lot of the diner.

She parted her lips and they moved in tandem, dropping to the armchair together, in an embrace tight enough to allow them to sit together in the wide seat. Zack's strong hands cupped her face and pulled her in harder. Too soon, their kiss ended, each equal parts satisfied and *un*satisfied. But, Becky realized, in a moment that would be awkward with a new person, such discomfort didn't exist between her and Zack. Even after two decades.

Especially after two decades.

But the question took shape. First on her mind then on her heart. Then her lips. "What's next?"

"Well," he began, scratching his flexed jawline as he glanced toward his bookshelf. "I have to know something before this goes anywhere, Becky."

She licked her lips and frowned. "Okay?"

"Are you staying in Hickory Grove?" A million questions hung between them, but he was starting with the most basic. Her stomach churned at her stalled job search. Memaw's bills piling up on the counter. The long-dead farm where she was raised. Her own future was uncertain.

"I want to," she answered, her eyes shifting away, exploring Zack's house. It wasn't chic or modern. It wasn't very big, either. For a lawyer's son who became a lawyer himself, he could have done better. But that wasn't Zack. It never had been. His dad had always complained that Zack wouldn't live up to his potential. That Zack could be great. Could be whatever he wanted and live wherever he wanted.

And Zack had chosen Hickory Grove. He'd chosen to work for the area schools, in a familiar career, but different. He'd chosen to be great. In his own way.

"But?" Zack answered, standing abruptly and moving toward the farm table that spread from the edge of the living room to the back wall. A neat row of casement windows sat above the table in an orderly, no-nonsense fashion.

She lifted her hands and let them fall again, clapping onto her upper thighs. Her hands stretched across the worn cotton fabric of Zack's oversized sweats. She could wear those every day for the rest of her life and be happy. She felt so at home in them. She'd never worn anything of Andrew's. It was a strange, happy feeling. "I need to figure out what I'm doing with my life. I have bills to pay. So does Memaw. I promised Theo I'd send him money. I want to stay, of course I do. Not just to help Memaw, either. Or to be close to Theo—" Now she was rambling. Her eyes flicked to his, and Zack cracked a smile. Becky had to look away. Her knees felt wobbly and she might sink into the chair if she held his gaze.

"I might be able to help with the job thing," he offered, rubbing at his jawline again. "But what about the schoolhouse? Aren't you going to pursue that?"

Becky's head snapped toward Zack, her face tense. "You're tearing it down."

"*I* was never tearing it down," he answered, his voice soft, his features hard. "I had suggested it before I knew you wanted it. The school agreed. The plans were set."

"*Why*, Zack? *Why?*" she asked as she gestured toward the book in his hands Maybe he didn't know if his mom went there. But he *must* have known it had a special place in her heart. He must have.

Zack swallowed. "I was trying to move on, Becky! The only way I knew how."

"By tearing down a piece of the past? The place your own mom went to school?" she pushed, anger bubbling in her throat. Welling in her eyes. It didn't matter that he hadn't known his own mother went there. It wasn't *her* fault his dad pretended the poor women had no history. It was *Zack's* fault for being so . . . *lawyery*.

"No!" he answered. "By tearing down the place that reminded me of you!"

She froze. Involuntarily, she began to shake her head. She couldn't understand him. His waffling between nostalgia and practicality. How he clung to the past but wouldn't even talk about his own mother. She stood and made a move for the door, ready to ignore him. This man who handled his issues by ignoring them. Pushing them away.

"Becky," he commanded, his voice cutting across the room. "Wait."

She did. Her face askance. Giving him one final chance.

He wiped his hand up across his face, but a frown still settled there. "Becky, I called Mr. Engelhard, and I asked him to cancel the demolition."

Chapter 20

Becky froze. "What?"

Zack took a step toward her, his hands lifted in apology, his face solemn. "I called the district and asked about the schoolhouse. I spoke with the superintendent. Mr. Engelhard."

She brought her hands to her mouth, and her face stretched in excitement. "No, I know. I got that much." A laugh escaped her mouth, and she searched his eyes for the good news. But it wasn't there. "What did he say, Zack?" Involuntarily, she moved closer to him, suddenly desperate.

In a matter of moments her entire future flashed through her head. She saw herself replacing floorboards and painting the siding, planting flowers. She saw herself order squat sets of classics and lining them along the chalkboard trays and in precious wooden shelves hewed from the original wooden desks.

She saw Theo visiting on his winter break and running the till while she went to grab them take-out lunch from Mally's. She even saw Zack meeting her at home after a long day of work. They would share a glass of wine in front of his fireplace—or hers.

She saw it all.

But as though he knew her mind, Zack shook his head sadly. "I'm so sorry, Becky. They, well, they're taking my word and moving forward. As long as the property belongs to the district, it has to go."

Her heart sank in an instant. A low throb crawled up the back of her neck.

Why had she come here, again?

Suddenly, her memory seemed to slip, and she took a step back. Zack reached for her but she held up her palm. "What do you mean they're taking *your* word?"

"I told you, Beck. The superintendent doesn't want the school to be liable if someone falls and gets hurt in there. Or if it becomes a public eyesore. It's cheaper to tear something down than to build it back up."

Everything Becky had pictured just moments ago came swirling back to her. Renovations, furniture, fresh stacks of books (used and new) adding their papery smell against the backdrop of a bustling-but-small shop. Becky's shop. Becky's little country book shop.

She squeezed her eyes shut.

"Becky," Zack pleaded. "I'm sorry." His hands dropped to his sides in defeat.

All of Becky's energy slipped out of her. She wanted to curl up in bed and sleep. For a long time.

"I have to go," she whispered, bending down to tug her satchel up over her shoulder. Zack watched as she shuffled to the front door. Turning, she gave him one last smile. She knew it would be the last. It had to. She would have to move now. She'd have to go to New Albany or Louisville where she could have a true fresh start. Because whatever she thought she was going to get here, back in Hickory Grove, well—she didn't get it. Instead, she got a dead grandfather and an ex-boyfriend who was still very much her ex.

She paused with her hand on the doorknob. "You know, Zack," she started, turning slowly, regaining a little of her energy. The anger pushed it through her.

His eyebrows lifted in answer. "What, Beck?" He asked at last.

"I thought you were better than that."

***

"His mom would be so disappointed in him," she spat.

Maggie glanced up from her manicure, a glob of nail polish hanging heavily from its miniature brush. "I hope you didn't say that to him."

"Not exactly." Becky reddened, regret seeping into her chest.

"Are you kidding me? Becky, you need a reality check. You're not living in a movie. People can't just cancel their plans because you roll back into town with some big idea. In real life, no one's dreams come true."

Becky pinched and unpinched her straw and stared over Maggie's shoulder toward the counter.

It was the next afternoon. Becky begged Maggie to join her for a soda at Mally's.

Maggie dropped Briar off with Memaw, which surprised Becky. She didn't realize how close they'd become over the years. But with her own mother and now her aunt dead, Maggie needed *someone*. Memaw liked being *someone*. Especially these days.

Maggie capped her nail polish and stowed it in her purse before fanning her hands across the Formica table. She had a bad habit of touching up her nails wherever she was, even if it was a public place where people were *eating*.

Becky sighed.

"Are you really going to beg Bill to hire you? *Here?*" Maggie's bottle-blonde hair sank around her face. Dark-liner smudged her lower lash line. She looked tired. Unwell, even.

"Who are you to judge?" Becky replied, eyeing her friend scornfully.

Maggie delicately dipped another fry in ranch dressing and ignored the look. "You're better than this town, Becky. You and Zack both. Why don't you two just run away to a bigger city? It'd suit you."

At that, Becky felt her face grow flush. She was proud of her hometown. She wasn't better than it. She wasn't better than anyone or anything. But she *wanted* better for it.

"Maggie, your kids go to school here," Becky pleaded.

Maggie rolled her eyes and dunked another fry.

Becky pressed on. "Don't *you* care about making it a great town? Don't *you* care about bringing out the best here? Maybe you're so busy complaining that you've forgotten to stop and open your eyes. You're just blindly . . . reacting to things. Just like the stupid school board and that harried superintendent. And Zack, too. They see a dilapidated building. An eyesore. A place where someone might get hurt and have cause to sue. But that isn't what I see."

Maggie swallowed down her last starchy fry and followed Becky's gaze as she peered out the smudged window. From her seat in the booth, she had a view to the best intersection in Indiana. The epitome of small-town U.S.A. A place she wouldn't nearly appreciate so much if she hadn't spent half her life somewhere else, probably.

Just outside the diner, Main Street crossed ways with Overlook Lane. Smackdab at the crossroads you could stop for gas and general goods in the corner market. You could deposit your babysitting check in Southern Indiana Credit Union. You could enjoy hearty grub in Mally's (even if it wasn't the exact same grub Mally used to fry up himself). You could duck into The Ice Cream Shoppe for a vanilla with sprinkles any day of the week.

And if you cared to venture fewer than a hundred yards, you'd wind up at Little Flock Baptist or St. Ann's Catholic Church for Sunday service.

And, if you had a mind to explore, you could stroll the grass-lined sidewalk up Overlook Lane and admire from a short distance beautiful Victorian-style homes that somehow made their way into Hickory Grove.

And if you *really* wanted to appreciate Hickory Grove, you'd turn back the other way, across rolling green hills and through thickets of hickory trees and oaks and maples and junipers until you found yourself in front of one of the oldest buildings that still stood in this old town: The Hickory Grove Schoolhouse.

But no one stopped for that stuff anymore.

Becky's mind travelled back in time to Friday nights. "Do you remember football games?" Becky murmured through her reverie.

Maggie let out a cackle. "Sure do. I got into more trouble under those dang bleachers." She slurped at her soda. "Remember Josh? Josh Privit? That was my first kiss, you know."

"I know," Becky answered, now smiling across the table. "I can't believe my mama let me hang out with you. You were bad, Maggie *Devereux*."

"Well, I'm not Maggie *Devereux* anymore." Sadness replaced the laughter in her eyes and she looked down at her soda.

Becky frowned. "I know. I'm just teasing you."

"Beck, I don't know who the heck I am." It caught them both by surprise. Sudden tears spilled over Maggie's black lashes, wetting her face like an unexpected monsoon.

"What do you mean? Maggie, are you okay?" Becky slid her hand across the table and gripped her friend's wrist, darting a glance around the diner.

Maggie wiped at her face and let out a sniffly chuckle. "Yeah, I'm fine. I just don't know what I was thinkin' when I married him. Or what I was thinking when I decided to stay here. It's not what I wanted to do. I don't know why the heck *you* want to stay around here. Becky, Theo's upstate. Your mom's in California. Even Ben lives somewhere else."

Becky shook her head. "I don't believe you, Mags. I don't believe you hate Hickory Grove. I don't believe you think I should move, either." She paused long enough to slice a finger at her blonde, broken friend. "This is about *you*. Your marriage. Leave Travis. Be done. Stop pulling everyone else into your train wreck. Hickory Grove has everything to offer you. A chance to be better. It's here. You're just not looking for it. You're looking for sympathy. I have none. You want this place to be better? You want to see the world? You're not going to do that by shaming the community in which you grew up. You do it by watering the grass. Volunteering in the school. Praying behind a wooden pew. Checking a book out of the library . . ." Becky stopped midsentence. It was a great lecture. One for the books. But that was just it. "Wait, Maggie. . ."

The shadow had cleared from Maggie's face. Sunlight brightening her freckles and highlighting her red roots. She was staring intently at Becky. Drinking in the words. Studying them. "What?"

"The library. What happened to Hickory Grove Library?" Becky had ridden her old bike all over town. She hadn't stopped in at the library. A place she'd known well as a child. It hadn't even occurred to her do so. How had she missed it?

Maggie's eyes were dry and wide. "Closed. We don't have one anymore. Even the school library is closed down. It was big drama. One of the English teachers loans out books, I think. Though I only know because . . ." she trailed off.

"Maggie, that's it!" Becky's voice lifted above the greasy mist that coated both their plates. She raised her hand toward the nameless waitress and asked for the check. "I'm going to open the schoolhouse. I'm going to make it a library. The school can't turn that down. What school board member or parent would vote against it?"

She was fumbling for change in her purse when Maggie tossed a twenty-dollar bill onto the Formica table and stood. "*I* don't know, but I *do* know someone who might be able to help."

Chapter 21

He couldn't help. Zack didn't know what the superintendent *or* the board would think about such a plan. The three of them were in Zack's in-home office.

Becky drummed her fingers across his broad, oak desk as Maggie stalked the bookshelf opposite. Both women had marveled at his second collection. Becky had wondered if that's where *The Wizard of Oz* might be hiding.

"So, what . . . you work—telepathically?" Maggie asked as she thumbed through an early edition of *Great Expectations*.

Zack laughed. "I *telecommute*. Sometimes, yes." He lifted and dropped his hands onto his desk. "Listen, Beck. I'll do whatever you want me to do. I'll call them up now and pitch the idea. But the problem is and always will be money. Starting a library means even more money, too. It's an expense, and the state of public education in America is such that *expenses* are highly frowned upon. I don't know if we'll have any luck."

She liked that he used *we*.

"Well, let's approach this productively, then. What's the best route? Should I write a letter to the board? Should I garner community support, first? Who would be against a historic library?" She batted her eyes and considered such suggestions. It might take a while. Weeks. Months. She'd need to find interim employment. She'd need to commit. To staying. In Hickory Grove.

"Garnering community support is helpful, yes. But it won't matter, Beck. The board would rather you host library services in the newer library. The one in the high school. It's currently used for lunch detention, but they could have that somewhere else, I'm sure. Anyway, my point is if you're goal is to resurrect a library, no one in the district will want to sink money into rehabbing the schoolhouse. It's too risky. Too pricey. You can go ask for yourself, but I'm telling you what I know."

Becky looked at Maggie, who'd reshelved *Great Expectations* and sank into an overstuffed leather chair. She returned Becky's knowing look with a shrug. "Let's try the board. I think they have meetings every month, right, Zack?"

Zack nodded gravely. "First Tuesday. There's a Call to the Public at the end of each meeting where community members can sign up to speak their piece. It's simple enough. Maybe they'll listen to you. Maybe if it comes from the person in question, they'll care."

Becky bit down on her lower lip. Zack's half-hearted attitude made her regret their kisses. Regret that she'd worn his outfit home and washed it, adding an extra teaspoon of fabric softener. What a waste. She swallowed. "Fine. First Tuesday of October is . . ." She hesitated, trying to do basic math in her head. Being out of work and away from her school-aged child had removed her from things like calendars.

"Tomorrow," Maggie answered, sighing. "It's tomorrow."

***

It was a strangely simple affair. Becky was nervous as all get-out. She'd opted for the yellow sundress she'd worn that first day she and Zack went for a walk. She wished she had something else. Something to tempt him into bribing the school board on her behalf. Something a little sexy and a little business all at once.

But the sundress looked nice on her. Cheery. It would have to do.

She'd applied light makeup and blew out her hair, but a distinct feeling of otherness overcame her as she climbed the wooden steps up to the second floor of the district office. The boardroom loomed at the end of the hall. Memaw followed close behind. Maggie was home with her kids. Becky had clear orders to call or text her as soon as she finished her spiel.

"I wonder if Zack'll be here," Memaw's voice bounced around the narrow hallway and Becky shushed her.

"Think of this like church, Memaw. These people take their jobs seriously, you know," Becky scolded.

Memaw laughed. "If that were true then they'd have a library!"

Warmth spread up Becky's neck. She wanted to laugh and cry all at once. But mostly, she wanted to walk in with Zack. She wanted to see him. To know he was on her side, fully. She wanted to start over and take back her anger with him. It wasn't Zack's fault about the schoolhouse. He said he'd tried. She believed that.

Once they stepped into the room, claustrophobia engulfed her. Four short rows of metal chairs lined the space in front of an expansive wooden cabinet. From the top of the cabinet, nine microphones sprouted. Behind each station was a dramatic headshot of, apparently, the board members, whose names appeared engraved on gold plates above each framed photograph.

An American flag hung limply in the corner next to Indiana's state flag. For such a small, cramped space, the attempt at formality felt disproportionate.

Becky and Memaw had arrived fifteen minutes early. Only three of the board members were seated and all three completely ignored the entrance of the two interlopers.

In the audience, if you could call it that, sat one lone man and, across the room, one lone woman. The heavy summer air pervaded the room through a rusty swamp cooler that hummed in a window, intermittently stalling then sputtering back to life.

Zack wasn't there yet.

Becky and Memaw shuffled into the narrow back row, each one easing into her chair as it creaked beneath.

Memaw leaned over to Becky as the board members continued to chat amongst themselves. "That one there went to school with your mom," Memaw whispered loudly as she pointed a crooked finger up at a silver-haired woman with false eyelashes. Becky shushed her again but wondered about all these contradictions. The stylish trio who represented a school that couldn't afford to keep a library in circulation. The posh headshots lining an outdated board roam wherein they attempted to cool a southern building with a swap unit in the thick of summer. Strange.

What caught Becky most by surprise was that she didn't know these people. These Hickory Grove locals who belonged on a corporate board rather than in a rural school district. Strange. All of it.

Becky thought of Theo and his southwestern upbringing. He was lucky to attend the best school district in Tucson, where the board members were largely irrelevant. Nothing hung in the balance. Everyone seemed more worried about getting kids to read and write and count and add than anything else.

But Tucson was lacking in other ways, of course. Specifically, any semblance of a fall, winter, or spring. Becky looked forward to leaves dropping from their trees in Hickory Grove, blanketing the town like an autumn-colored cashmere throw.

Slowly, the remaining board members trickled in. Some looked like they'd spent the day at the town's nine-hole, par-three golf course. Some came straight from work, wherever that was. One probably rolled in from supper with her family. Becky liked that one best. Then, together, the last three attendees turned up.

Mr. Engelhard.

His long-suffering secretary, whose name was as forgettable as her outfit.

And Zachary Durbin, Esquire.

Becky's breath hitched when she saw him.

Of course, Zack spotted her as soon as he passed.

Just before he took his seat next to the secretary, he turned and threw her another of his heart-melting winks.

Becky smiled back, her lips quivering in nervous energy.

Maybe everything would go her way tonight. Maybe the board would say *yes,* and then Becky could say *yes* to Zack. After all, wasn't this whole ordeal the one thing that kept her from falling into his arms every night? Whether she had something to stay for or not? A future?

She glanced at Memaw out of the corner of her eye. If things didn't work, Becky would simply have to drag the old woman with her. From their home to a place with more opportunity. A place where she wouldn't have to face her high school sweetheart when she was at the corner shop in her pajamas on a Sunday morning.

Becky kept her gaze on Zack. He wore a suit—a suit that fit him with immaculate precision. A suit that was made for a body like Zack's. Long and lean with broad shoulders and muscular legs. A firm butt.

Becky forced herself to breathe through the nerves, rummaging in her satchel for the speech she'd written.

The proceedings began, first with the Pledge of Allegiance, then with a moment of silence. Afterwards, both Mr. Engelhard's secretary and one of the board members muttered an Amen.

Even with the unfamiliar faces, Becky had to admit that it felt like home.

Now and again Zack would glance back at Becky and smile. Once, he nodded, as if to spur her on. It worked. Over the course of listening in on budgetary spending and hiring approvals, her confidence grew.

By the last agenda item (a discussion on parking passes for high school students), Becky could again visualize her new life. It included Memaw and the farm, Zack and his pretty Victorian house, and her working out of the schoolhouse—at least in some capacity. Preferably as a book shop. Possibly as an interim librarian as she worked on finishing her degree. Maybe.

"All right, then," the superintendent's voice droned from behind the cabinet. "Last item is the Call to Public. Anyone may have the floor for a timed total of two minutes. The Call to the Public may not include discussion on matters pertaining to executive board agenda items, of which we have none for this month, anyway. Speakers must act respectfully. Who do we have first?"

The dowdy-looking older woman who sat near the useless swamp cooler stood and smoothed her skirt down. She lifted a firm hand toward the board and offered a curt wave. It wasn't until that awkward half-salute that Becky recognized her.

"Fern Gale," the woman offered as a robotic introduction. When a few of the board members nodded her on skeptically, she spoke from a crumpled piece of notebook paper. "I tried to address this matter di-rectly with the town council but they referred me here." Her voice rattled. She paused to clear her throat. "The Christmas tree-lighting event is coming up."

A snicker rose from somewhere behind the cabinet. Becky searched for its source, but every single one of the board members were suspect. Exasperation mixed with amusement in their expressions. *So much for respect.*

The poor woman tried again. "Anyway, last year, y'all were so—well, I heard that . . . that it almost didn't happen. So I'm wondering if y'all are gonna have the Christmas tree-lighting ceremony this year. And if so, well I'd like to help." Her voice finally cracked and she whooshed into her seat. Becky cringed. The poor woman was painfully uncomfortable. Surprisingly, it did little to garner any sympathy.

"That's a matter for the town council," the board president boomed back, as though Fern were hard of hearing.

Fern nervously glanced around the room. Becky wanted to step in for her, but her own confidence was slipping quickly, and she really needed that board to side with her.

Fern stood again, this time visibly shaking. She started to open her mouth to clarify (unnecessarily), but Zack shot up.

"May I address the board?" His voice was firm and commanding. He wasn't asking a question, he was offering a direction. The president and the rest of the board nodded back. "It's obvious Ms. Gale already went to the town council."

Memaw nudged Becky, and the two women shared a smile. Poor Fern simply stared at Zack.

"We don't handle the tree lighting, Mr. Durbin," Mr. Engelhard cut in. "You know that."

"If she already went there, then her question is for *you*." Zack sat and propped his ankle over his opposite knee in a wide, relaxed position. The secretary glanced back at Becky this time, as if to warn her. Becky looked away, resting her gaze on Fern, who again had her eyes on the floor.

Zack's intrusion was completely inappropriate, technically. According to the agenda, the speaker during the call to public had the floor exclusively. It was a way to prevent a mob from coming in and attacking the board.

Becky's confidence was again bolstered. He'd do the same for her. She felt her face cool and was able to focus on Fern.

"The ceremony can only happen with volunteers, and all the school clubs typically do that. They set it up and run the thing, you know." She faltered but pushed on. "Well, the council told me they weren't volunteering last year so it didn't happen. I'd just like to see if I could act as a, uh, a liaison or somethin' to help with that." Again she sat, this time with something of a thud.

Becky watched the board for their reaction. Everyone's eyes fell on the president who nodded slowly. "We'll add to next month's agenda as a discussion item." He clapped his hands once as if the matter was solved. "Next?" Fern sank deeper into her seat, but a small sigh escaped her mouth and curled across the room. The world's tiniest rebellion. Becky liked her.

Everyone looked at the other gentleman in attendance, expecting him to take the floor. Indeed, he stood. But instead of addressing the board, he scuttled down his row and escaped through the back door. Bizarre as could be.

"Okay, then," the president said. "Maybe he wasn't ready." The board laughed derisively, stunning Becky into standing.

She swallowed and blinked hard, pressing ahead. "I'm next, then."

The superintendent whispered something to the president who dipped his head toward Becky.

Zack turned and smiled, nodding once again.

Her knees buckled, but she righted herself and took a breath. "My name is Rebecca Linden. I was born and raised in Hickory Grove, but I left for college years ago." She didn't have to mention that she never finished college. This was all about credibility and authority. She needed that degree. "I'm back in town and hoping to—well, I'm planning to lay down my roots here once again." A glance toward Memaw revealed the old woman to be shooting lasers at the board members.

The president grumbled something and waved his hand to prod her on. Becky returned her eyes to her speech and read carefully. "I've always held great affection for the little schoolhouse that sits at the far end of Overlook Lane. My grandfather and grandmother attended school there. I played there as a girl." A thought occurred to her that she probably shouldn't have mentioned that. It was fuel for the *attractive nuisance* argument. Too late now. "I'd like to see about renovating the building. I'd be happy to pitch in. One day, maybe it could even act as the school library. Or maybe you could sell it to me. Or lease it." She'd gone off-script.

The president dipped his head toward the others, whose faces were blank, as though they didn't even know there *was* a schoolhouse. The president answered her. "In accordance with local, state, and federal funding, the board is unable to resurrect the library services for the district. It's a shame, we know." The line of middle-aged *public servants* all nodded in solemn agreement. "Tragic, even. But there you have it." He laced his fingers and propped them at the edge of his podium.

Becky lifted her hand to rebuttal but didn't wait for approval. She could feel Zack shifting in his seat. "Well, perhaps you might sell it or rent it out?" she asked, hating that her voice floated into impossibly high octaves.

"Can you buy it from us today? Do you have cash on hand?" The president redirected. A sneer creeping across his pale, thin lips.

Becky looked at Memaw, who sat helpless, then shook her head. His sneer escalated into a smile and he raised his hands. "We have a contract out for demo. It'll be razed next week, I do believe. Ain't that right, Zack?" The president's formal language dipped all the way into improper grammar, and Becky glared at the back of Zack's head.

He stood. "President Mackay, Becky here—er, *Ms. Linden* might like to know if you can delay the plans and reconsider. The schoolhouse *is* a historical building."

"When did you become the public *liaison*, Mr. Durbin?" One of the other board members piped up, her eyes hard.

Mr. Engelhard cleared his voice and entered the conversation. "Zack, you can't speak on behalf of the public, even to clarify."

Zack sat back down and nodded dutifully. Becky thought she heard him apologize.

She raised her voice. "I'd like to know if you can delay the plans and reconsider." Memaw nudged her in affirmation.

The president chuckled and looked at Zack. "Well, Mr. Durbin, in your professional opinion as a litigator and our legal representative, I think you can answer this question here and now." The room grew still and quiet. The swamp cooler hummed more quietly. Cool air began to pump forth as though the outside temperature suddenly dropped twenty degrees. Becky shivered.

"Go ahead, sir," Zack answered, his voice unwavering.

"Mr. Durbin, is the schoolhouse an—aw heck, what did you call it? An 'attractive lure' or whatever?" Becky was floored by his air quotes as much as by his language. The whole tone of this meeting appalled her.

"An attractive nuisance, sir." Zack answered, correcting him.

"Oh, right. Is the schoolhouse an attractive nuisance? Might someone get hurt there? Say, a little girl who stumbles upon it and drags her collection of Barbie dolls inside?" The man had the gall to smile at Becky.

She forced herself to match his smile then watched Zack, awaiting his reply. She felt ready for this fight. Nervous, but ready.

Zack darted a quick glance back at her then turned his head again and took a moment before he answered.

"Well, Zack? Is it a danger?" The president pressed.

Zack cleared his throat and then replied. "Yes."

"So Ms. Linden, you don't have the money, and that building is currently a danger to the public. Our only option is to follow Mr. Durbin's original advice and tear the dang thing down. Zack, Ms. Linden, have I got that right?" All the board members were smirking now.

Becky felt heat grow up her neck. Memaw grabbed her hand. The old woman began to stand and say something, but Becky pulled her back down and shushed her again. Everyone seemed to wait. And then Zack finally answered.

"Yes, sir. You're right." he said.

Chapter 22

Becky had torn out of the boardroom, leaving Memaw in her wake only to have to wait awkwardly at the truck until the old woman had managed to catch up. Once Memaw appeared at the entrance, Becky saw Zack behind her, holding the door.

Chivalry couldn't save him now.

She stared hard, daring Zack to approach her. He began to follow Memaw, but she turned and said something to him. The exchange was calm and left Zack with a sad slump in his shoulders.

Becky didn't care.

"We have to move out of Hickory Grove, Memaw," Becky said once they were buckled in and pulling out of the parking lot. "There's nothing for us here."

"Oh, bull honkey. Your mother tried the same dramatics years ago. You know where that got her?"

Becky didn't. She shook her head, fighting back tears.

"It got her to California with a loser boyfriend who won't commit and a job she hates," Memaw spat.

A frown fell across Becky's mouth. "I thought she was happy. All she ever wanted was to leave Hickory Grove. See the world. Relive her lost youth or whatever."

"She wanted happiness, Rebecca. Happiness. And she figured an escape would make her happy. Running away from her problems. She thought that if she could just stay with you two until you graduated, that she had completed her obligation and could move on. What your mother didn't think about was how it'd make her feel."

Confusion and hurt welled in Becky's chest, and a tear slipped down her cheek. "I knew we were a burden. I didn't know she wanted to get away from us."

"No, no. Now don't you go making a mountain out of a molehill. You were hard on your mom but not because of who you were. Because of who *she* was. Your mom didn't know who she was. So running away seemed like a good plan. She might find herself. I don't think she ever has." A heavy pause filled the truck cab as it heaved up the hill toward the farm.

Once Becky had parked in the gravel drive, both women sat. A thoughtful silence swirled around them for several moments.

"I know who I am," Becky murmured, at last.

Across the bench seat Memaw creeped her wrinkled hand, covering Becky's. Her skin was soft and warm. Becky looked down through the darkness and then back out. Memaw squeezed her frail fingers around the back of her granddaughter's hand. "Becky, that's why you have to stay and fight."

***

"She's right. You love that dumb schoolhouse, and you love books, and you love your Memaw. And me, by the way," Maggie droned over a phone call the next morning.

Becky was getting changed out of an old pair of overalls she'd found. They were her mom's gardening overalls. They still smelled like Patsy, even. Laundry soap and lavender. Becky had a job interview in New Albany. Finally. It was a secretarial position with the New Albany Unified School District. Not quite irony. More like fate. Becky was destined to deal with the school system for the rest of her life, probably. In some way or another.

"I know. I know. But I have to have money, Mags. I have to have an income. Theo called earlier."

Maggie waited a beat before pressing. "*And?*"

"And he got a part-time job," Becky began. "But he gave me a tally of his monthly expenses. He's been using my credit card until now. We think his new job will cover food at least. His scholarship covers tuition. But that still leaves the dorm, textbooks, and anything else that comes up. I've charged everything until now, and I'm about to be hit with a colossal credit card bill."

"Can Memaw help until you figure things out?" Maggie asked.

"No way. I'm not asking for that. She's on a fixed income. I won't go there, Maggie, come on." Becky scrunched her hair and rubbed a layer of sunscreen over her face. "I'm heading into town soon. I have an interview."

"*Town* town?" Maggie asked. *Town* town meant New Albany.

"Yep. New Albany Unified. It's a start, at least. And the timing is perfect. It's as if they had a mole at the school board meeting who was setting a trap. *Make sure she doesn't get what she wants in Hickory Grove! She's perfect for filing papers and calling parents of absentee students.*" The women laughed into the phone together.

"Well, break a leg, I guess. What about Zack?"

Becky froze in the mirror. She'd begun to add mascara, opting for a natural look. At his name, her hand slipped and she smeared her brush across her upper cheek.

"What about him? I think our relationship is clear. He sided against me. With *them*. I can't date him. It would sicken me, Maggie." Maggie didn't respond. Dead air filled Becky's ear. "He didn't even call me or text after what happened last night."

"It's his job, Beck." Maggie's voice was quiet on the other end of the line.

Becky scoffed. "If he's so committed to his job that he can't stand up for what's right, then it won't work. See? This is exactly my point." She wiped off the mascara smudge and finished her lashes.

"I don't think that's the point at all, actually. I think this whole mess shows that he's a careful person. He tries to do what *is* right, in fact. Becky, you are the only person in this whole town who ever cared about that darn ol' building. And you showed up out of the blue with a different idea than anyone else."

When Becky didn't say anything in reply, Maggie let out a sigh. "You know what, Rebecca? You're still stubborn as the day you left. I gotta go. Good luck at your *interview*."

The sound of nothing took the place of Maggie's breathy voice.

Was *everyone* against her? Memaw's warning about dramatics pounded in her heart and she shook off the slight.

Maggie loved Zack as much as anyone. She thought they belonged together. She thought Zack was perfect, but Maggie had low standards.

If Zack were perfect, he would always have wanted that schoolhouse to stay standing. He wouldn't be a litigious jerk who feared the worst. A coward. Who didn't give two hoots about his heritage.

Then again, Becky knew she was stubborn. Maggie wasn't wrong.

She slid the mascara brush back into its tube and screwed the top then tossed it back onto the bathroom counter and checked her watch. She had two hours before her interview. New Albany was a two-and-a-half-hour drive.

It was time to go.

***

As Becky rolled out of the drive and down the hill onto Main Street toward the fork, Maggie's words replayed in her head.

The only person in this whole town who ever cared about that darn building.

It wasn't true. Memaw and Grandbern cared about it, for starters. She even promised them she'd revive it. Turn it into something. Letting the promise slip through the fingers of municipal hogwash felt slimy and horrid.

But they weren't the only ones who cared.

Darla Durbin.

A little girl's shakey script flashed through Becky's mind as her car tipped up, nearing the fork. Just before she came to a complete stop, she stared out over the green pastures, beyond Mally's and the corner shop to her place.

Her schoolhouse.

She had only days left. Demo would start soon. Maybe they'd let Becky keep some of the scrap. She could make something out of it, like Zack had.

How shameful. A historic building, a one of-its-kind in this country . . . whittled down into a book end or centerpiece. A fraction of its greatness.

Then, as she came to a full, sad stop at the four-way, color caught her eye. Shiny silver peeked out from the far side of the schoolhouse.

Someone was there.

Please don't let it be the construction crew already, Becky prayed silently.

She swallowed hard and glanced at the clock. Time was ticking away. Even if she sped over there now, she wouldn't have time to properly ask questions or stall the process. She wouldn't have time to demand scraps for some useless arts and crafts project.

If she didn't drive through the four-way stop, she'd be late for her interview.

So Becky did the only thing she could. The thing she ought to have done eighteen years ago.

She followed her heart.

Chapter 23

Becky said prayer after prayer as she turned right onto Overlook and hummed down the dirt road. Pillows of dust billowed out from around her car.

The closer she got the more the vehicle at the schoolhouse became obscured, fading slowly behind the building. Out of sight.

As the clock on her dash ticked well into the hour, Becky's interview fell further to the back of her mind. All that mattered was saving her schoolhouse. Grandbern's schoolhouse. Memaw's schoolhouse. *Darla Durbin's* schoolhouse. Visions of her body lying prone in front of a bulldozer flashed across her brain as she parked along Overlook, at the end of the overgrown drive that once beckoned little children up to the front stoop.

Becky sat in the car and watched for movement. Thick ropes of greenery climbed up and across the mottled left window pane. The one on the right had long since blown out, but it revealed nothing since a fat, patchy bush had crept far up the right side of the building and toward the sinking eaves.

Studying the exterior, it didn't appear to be under any sort of preparation for demolition. No spray-painted markings to signify water or electric lines.

Then again, there wouldn't be any. As far as she knew, the schoolhouse never had running water or electric. Instead, school children were responsible for working the water pump in the back field to bring in a few buckets a day. Water for washing up. Water for mopping the floors at the end of the school day.

And electric was entirely unnecessary. The east side of the schoolhouse was a wall of windows, now awash in broken shards of glass and all-consuming weeds and vines. Grandbern had told her that they depended on the sun to light their schoolwork. And, of course, a wood-burning stove was the source of heat during the winter time.

Grandbern had also told her it was his favorite thing about school. Chopping wood in the summer, stacking it, and then hauling it in each day. He felt like a man even when he was just a boy.

Maybe that's what Becky loved about the schoolhouse. It was living proof of the way things were. Children had real responsibilities then. They mattered. Adults *needed* them.

She knew her perspective was romanticized. She knew it. But it didn't change the way Becky felt.

She blinked and opened her car door, easing herself onto a patch of dirt. Her dress shoes, low-heeled clogs, instantly grew a coat of silt as she moved onto fall-grayed grass. For September, it sure felt like winter was near.

Her eyes trained on the building, she began to wonder if it wasn't a construction foreman or some sort of assessor who was staking out his next project, but instead a wanderer like her. Maybe someone, for once, stopped to admire the beauty in the decrepit, sinking little house.

Still no movement from within. Becky thought about hollering out, but a strange hollow feeling kept her silent. Was it anxiety over ignoring the clock (and therefore her interview)? Anxiety over running into an enemy? Someone who agreed with the town that this place ought to be condemned for once and for all?

Was a bad man inside? Trashing the place for good measure? No.

Maybe no one was inside. Becky was now standing directly in front of the crumbled stoop and still she heard nothing. Taking Memaw's age-old advice, she opted to make a circle first.

She made a right and began to pick through the tall, dry grass and toward the back door, dying for a peek inside before she had to confront whoever it was in a nondescript vehicle. Whoever had an interest in this place. *Her* place.

Momentarily, Becky forgot about the fact that someone else was there. Instead, she examined the building, drinking in what might be her last memory of it.

Deep green ivy led her across the broad side of the school. Traces of what was once probably a wooden bench sat in a rotted clump at her feet. Becky had never spent a lot of time on the outside of the schoolhouse. Mostly, she and Maggie had played inside. And of course, when Zack joined her here for their few rendezvous, they'd typically dash from his truck to the door and tuck away inside before anyone could spot them.

It had always made Zack nervous. Like they would get in trouble for trespassing.

"How can it be trespassing if no one really owns it?" Becky would always argue, despite the fact that she knew it belonged to the school district. She wasn't one to trespass to begin with, but she never felt like the schoolhouse was off-limits. She'd practically grown up inside of it. And everyone who knew her knew she spent time there.

But Zack was a rule follower by his very nature.

"Becky, somebody *owns it,"* he'd say with ominous emphasis on the *"somebody."*

Then, as if he figured he'd never go back to Hickory Grove, he'd agreed to have that last picnic. The one which pushed them so far apart. And for so long.

Now, as she came to a stop near the back door, just around the corner from the mysterious vehicle, she realized Zack had been right all along.

This place never belonged to her.

The door fell into the building, leaving Becky to believe the stranger was there. Inside. Walking past the door was futile. She had to confront the person. Maybe she'd even have a shot at convincing them to delay. Give her a chance to rob a bank so she could buy it from the school.

Something. Anything.

At the very least, she had her opening to say goodbye.

She checked her wrist watch. If there was any hope in salvaging her interview, she would literally have to dip in and out then speed recklessly to New Albany. *And* she would have to call them and beg for mercy if she wound up late. Which she likely would.

Or, she could skip it. Stay here. Nag Bill at the diner until he gave her something. Send a resume to the bank. Elsewhere.

Fear and indecision struck together like a lightning storm in the pit of her stomach. She had to go. There was no way she could sit around town and wait for nothing.

Becky pressed her hand to her mouth and then transferred a kiss to the siding of the school.

This was goodbye.

She swallowed hard, a useless tear collecting on the inside of her eye. Becky tried to think about the future. About anything else. She tried to form a plan in which she'd simply swing by on the day of the demo, grab a piece of rotted schoolhouse and be on her way. Happy to have a fragment. She'd move on. She'd moved on from heartache before. And it got her Theo.

Theo. The boy who needed her most. The boy who needed his mom to stop worrying about him. About how he'd make it through school on little more than Notre Dame's expectation that he keep good grades.

He needed her money, probably. But mostly, he needed his mom to stand up and live her life.

She stepped back from the schoolhouse, but the heel of her clog caught on a piece of the shriveled, old bench and she went sailing backward, into half a foot of weedy grass.

Landing with a thump, she cried out with pain.

"Hello?" A man's voice called from within the schoolhouse.

Well, there went the interview. She'd be late for sure. They wouldn't hire her, and she'd be stuck right back where she was. "I'm fine!" Becky called back, pushing herself up and brushing off her bottom before trying to limp back to her car.

"Becky?"

Her pain dissolved, and she swiveled around like a top.

It wasn't a construction foreman. It wasn't a stranger. It was Zack.

Chapter 24

"What are you doing here?" Becky asked, feeling awkward in her interview outfit which by now was peppered in dirt and dead blades of grass.

Zack smiled and held up a small, battered book. She squinted through the morning sun.

The Wizard of Oz.

"Found it." His grin gave way to a frown. "Are you okay? Did you take a fall?"

Becky smiled in spite of herself. "Yeah. I'm fine." Her smile turned genuine as a memory tugged inside her head. "I think I remember that book, now that I see it. I didn't realize you had lost it. I'm sorry." She took a careful step toward him, studying the battered cover. "Yeah, that's it. Maggie and I played with it when we were girls. Where did you find it?" She desperately wanted to hold it. Maybe that was a better option than salvaging the rotten old wood. Maybe she'd come loot the place first. She glanced at her wrist watch. Anxiety crawled across her stomach, cramping it hard.

Zack waved behind him. "I dug around for a while. It was wedged between the teacher's desk and the wall. I don't know even know why I was looking so dang hard." A chuckle fell from his mouth and he turned the paperback in his hands. "My mom's name isn't in it. I double-checked."

"I'm sorry." Becky wasn't sure how else to reply. He took a step back and opened his body so that she could see into the door.

"Wanna come in?" He held his free hand toward her.

But she stayed in place, again glancing down at her watch. "I wish I could. I have an interview in New Albany. I'm going to be late. I have to go."

Zack nodded. Still, Becky stayed in place, her anxiety softening as she considered skipping the interview. It would be entirely unlike her. Out of character. A 180 degree change. Becky needed the job. She needed to know that Theo could make it through four years (or more) at Notre Dame without a looming pile of school loans to greet him come graduation.

But as she stood there, outside the schoolhouse with her old boyfriend on an otherwise perfect day, justifications for ditching the interview kicked in. *There was no sense in commuting to New Albany. She'd have to move. Would Memaw even agree to that?*

Memaw had ignored Becky when she shared the news of the interview.

That morning, Becky found the town newspaper strategically left on her dresser. It was folded open to the classifieds, of which there were more than she'd expected. Lots of animals for sale. Some livestock, some too-tempting-to-resist puppy litters. Two entire columns-worth of odds and ends. A page of automotives and heavy machinery, including farm equipment. And a good half-a-page of job listings.

Becky had been shocked to see places that were either brand new or that she had entirely forgotten.

Dollar Land. Becky scoffed.

Farm and Ranch Supply Co. Becky highlighted.

Hickory Hair and Nails. Becky texted Maggie.

Two new fast food joints had opened up on the far end of Main Street near the high school. Becky had zero interest in working fast food. At her age, it would be downright unhealthy. Fries for breakfast and milkshakes for dinner. No thanks.

Now, as she stood outside with the sun beating down on her black slacks and dark blouse, her stomach lurched in hunger. What she wouldn't give for fresh carrots from Memaw's garden. Warm rolls with a buttery center. Straight out of the oven.

A faint feeling crept up her neck and made her head feel swollen. Becky swayed a little, lifting her hand up to her eyes to shield the sun. Its rays had become overpowering. Black spots filled her vision and she squeezed them shut, her body again lurching left and right.

"Becky, come here." Zack's firm voice cut through the white noise that filled her ears. "You don't look well," he said as she felt him catch her at the waist and pull her into his body. He began to walk her into the schoolhouse, but her feet tripped along like a bow-legged baby doll's.

In a moment, he tucked a hand beneath her black slacks and lifted her high in the air, effortlessly. She felt light as a feather, and Zack ducked inside the low-hung door frame. He paused briefly until deciding on the teacher's chair where he set her down delicately. "Becky, try to take a few deep breaths, okay? Have you eaten anything today?"

With her head wedged into the crook of her arm as it pressed down on the desk, Becky murmured, "No. Too nervous."

She felt one of his hands press into her lower back. His breath and voice came close to her ear. "Just try to breathe. Maybe you have low blood sugar. I can drive you to Mally's if you want. Or home? Let's get some food in you, okay?"

She pulled up, pushing the pads of her thumbs into her temples to rub the dull ache away. It didn't work, but she felt herself regain color and energy. She felt better. A lot better. "I'm fine."

He nodded and let his hand slip away from her. She instantly missed it. And in that moment, Becky realized everything she had given up in the last eighteen years. Someone to take care of her. Someone other than Theo to show her love.

The love of a child was special. No question. But Becky needed the love of a partner. Someone on equal footing who had to *choose* to love her. Not be naturally disposed.

Perhaps more than any of that, she missed the touch of a man. A real man. A man who was gentle and kind. Careful and thoughtful.

A man like Zack, of course.

"Why are you interviewing in New Albany?" His voice cracked. Becky looked up, rubbing her hands along her thighs and licking her lips.

"I have to find something, Zack. Money is a stressor right now. Memaw can cover her own needs. But I can't expect her to cover mine. Plus, there's Theo." She felt a blush creep up her cheeks. She hated to admit all this to Zack, who had never had to worry about money in his entire life. He wouldn't understand. Maybe he wouldn't even care.

"I get it," he replied, squeezing into one of the student desks in front of her.

Becky ignored the pacifying fib and inspected the schoolhouse, her eyes passing over the familiar furniture. The empty wood stove that anchored the building. She couldn't imagine a bulldozer coming in and razing this whole place. Her heart began to hurt.

Her eyes fell on Zack, and she caught his gaze. His sad smile. And then she realized something. "Everything is as it always was, Zack," she began. "How come you thought it was a problem? Why did it even come up as an idea to take this place down? What happened?"

He blew out a sigh. "It wasn't just me, Beck."

She waited, unconvinced. Her eyes searched the room again, finding, miraculously, a distinct lack of evidence that anyone hung around here other than her. Even Maggie hadn't returned and she lived here. In Hickory Grove. A little town trying to grow. "I saw in the paper some new businesses," she said, changing the subject but only tangentially.

"Yeah, well. Some things do change." He answered. His face had dropped.

She figured other people in the community were ready to see the schoolhouse go. She had been in denial about that. But it made sense. And now he confirmed it. The mayor came to mind. Probably the wealthier people who lived far up Overlook Lane. Even higher than Zack. Or those whose estates were tucked behind the iron gates in Hickory Grove Manor. They preferred new to old. Landscaped to wild. Safety to danger.

Becky chuckled in spite of herself.

"What's so funny?" Zack asked, desperation in his eyes.

She shook her head. "Nothing." Then thought better of it. "Well, okay, Zack. I'll tell you what's so funny." She unleashed on him. "That you and the school board and the superintendent and everybody around here think of this place as some kind of threat!" She couldn't stop herself. "That it's dangerous. Or a nuisance. That someone would come here and get hurt and it would be *your* fault. Like you're scared. And you're not even scared that it could be a danger. You're scared of what could be. You always were. You were scared of what could be. And you still are. You fear the worse. You don't hope for the best. You don't see potential. You don't take risks. You worry. And I hate it." Tears stung her eyes, and Becky swallowed hard, her nostrils flaring. Screw everything. Screw manners and delicacy. Screw any shadow of hope she'd clung to over the past two decades. She had to have it out with Zack. Because she couldn't help Memaw or Theo or anyone if she didn't finally address this. Her feelings. *Their* feelings.

A look of shock froze Zack's features. Slowly, his face melted into a frown. A hateful frown. The same look of distaste he'd given her when she suggested he go to the UofA instead of Notre Dame. That he give up his own dream for hers.

When he said nothing, she simply shook her head, stood, and pushed the wooden chair back across the floor boards.

She didn't give him a chance to reply and instead stormed across the creaking wood and out into the knee-high grass and up to her car. As soon as she made it there, she heard his voice call after her.

"Stop right there!" he shouted. He was following, closing on her. She opened the door in time for him to grab it and hold it. His strength overpowered her. She sat and stared through the windshield, but he pushed himself into the gap and stared down at her from above.

"Becky, you pretend like history matters. You pretend that you care about Hickory Grove more than anyone else here. You pretend that it belongs to you and you alone." She kept her eyes ahead, trying hard to ignore him. But it was impossible. He didn't stop. "Becky Linden, if you cared so much, then why did you leave? Why didn't you come back?" His voice broke and lowered. "You don't care. *We* do."

And with that, he slammed the door shut and took back off toward the schoolhouse, disappearing inside.

Becky's lower lip quivered hard. Tears began to fall across her cheeks, but she did nothing to wipe them away. Instead, she grabbed her cell phone and dialed an unassigned phone number from her call log.

The voice that answered felt foreign and strange. Icy cold and decidedly unwelcome. "New Albany Unified School District, this is Martha."

Becky swallowed hard and cleared her throat, her tears retreating instantly as she shifted into survival mode. "Martha, hi. This is Rebecca Linden. I have an interview scheduled for this morning. Can you connect me with whoever is running it?"

Chapter 25: 1996

Becky was angry. Really angry.

Shocked that Zack had admitted it was okay to run away from hard stuff, she had to protect herself: by signing UofA's scholarship offer, shoving it into a thin, white envelope, slapping a stamp on top and popping it in the post office box in front of the corner shop.

Not even her own mailbox. She didn't want to take a chance. She couldn't hang her humility on an unreliable rural mail carrier. It had to go straight to the big blue box. It'd be safer. And, she couldn't change her mind in twenty minutes and dig it back out.

"The UofA?" Zack asked now, as they sat on her front porch. He'd shown up that evening, full of remorse over their argument.

She wasn't having it. It was a matter of values. Zack had been raised by a man who was scared to deal with things. She wasn't too naive to see the bigger picture.

"Are you sure?" he asked, shifting in the plastic chair across from the porch swing.

Becky kicked herself back into a full swing. "Yeah. I have to go where I can afford to." Her cheeks burned red. It was the first time she'd spoken about her money situation with Zack.

Obviously she was poor. He could see that plain as day. Her mom was a waitress. Her grandparents were farmers. She never got new clothes. All money went to keeping the farm alive. Even when the crops or the animals had a bad year, her family wasn't one to give in. They pushed on. Knowing their hard work would be rewarded. Tradition and work ethic were all that mattered to the Lindens.

Zack Durbin would never understand being poor. His dad was a lawyer with his own law practice. They lived in a beautiful home in Hickory Grove Manor. That Zack even went to the same school was purely because there was only *one* school in town.

"So you're just going to leave Indiana, then? How will you even get to Arizona?" Humor sliced through his words and Becky stopped the swing, ready with her answer.

"Maybe you can drive us. Maybe you can go to the UofA, Zack. You were accepted. It's an option, right?"

Zack fidgeted in his seat. "I wanted to go to the same school as you, Beck." He didn't look at her as he said it. She waited for him to finish. He didn't.

"But . . ." she added for him, her throat slowly closing as her eyes danced over her boyfriend. His cornflower blue polo with the little alligator on its breast. His khaki shorts and white sneakers. Self-conscious, she tucked her fingers into the threadbare patch on her jeans. Really she ought to cut it further open so it looked like she bought them that way. She was dumb.

"But you chose the UofA." He stood abruptly, hurt filling his eyes. She didn't understand.

"Zack, what do you mean?" She stood, too, her eyes flashing to the window by the front door. No one inside was watching.

They were totally alone. They could kiss and make up right then and there if they wanted.

A thought occurred to her. "Is this because of your dad?" she asked. "Does he think Notre Dame is a better school?" Before that moment, Becky hadn't put two and two together. In her mind, all universities were prestigious. And she took great pride in receiving an offer from one so far away. It meant something to her. She couldn't even remember how she'd ever heard of the school. Must have been her high school counselor's idea. Shame crossed through her heart.

Zack's dad had probably made the decision for him. When Zack didn't answer, she pressed again. "Did your dad choose your college?"

Zack sank back into his seat, defeated. He averted his gaze and shook his head. "I did, Beck."

"You're picking a better college over me." It was more a revelation than an accusation. Becky's legs felt weak and rubbery. She desperately wanted to run away from this embarrassment. This cut to her honor. But she physically couldn't. Instead, she sank back onto the swing and tucked her legs up under herself with one arm clinging to the back of it so she could stare far away from him.

"It has nothing to do with you, Becky. It's just that—" he blew a sigh out of his mouth and shifted audibly in the plastic chair. "It's where my parents went to college. That's all."

She didn't know what she hated more. That he chose this very moment to finally mention his mom or that his future choices had nothing to do with her. She snorted, ignoring his declaration. She refused to take the bait. "Okay," was all she had left in her.

Becky loved Zack. She wanted to marry him and have children with him and raise those children here—in Hickory Grove. Maybe they could even start a farm. Maybe they could buy the land next to the schoolhouse and ask the district to open it back up and have a little kindergarten there. Maybe Becky could become a kindergarten teacher and Zack could work the land and do lawyer stuff as a part-time job.

Her hopes dissolved into deep-seated fears. Images of Zack partying up-state hurtled through her head. And all for what? His parents' legacy. Parents who weren't even together anymore. Becky knew she was being a selfish brat. She should be nice. Fair. She should be happy for him that he could fulfill some sort of fancy family tradition.

But she wasn't. She was afraid. "You'll find someone else there."

"No, I won't," he answered, his eyes finding hers. "I promise, Beck. I won't. We will call each other every night. I'll come visit you when I can."

Becky shook her head. "Did you already sign? Did you already decide for sure?"

She could see Zack swallow, his eyes downcast. "I thought I could convince you to go with me. I really did."

Anger crawled up her throat. "Well that was dumb. I guess you don't get it, then."

"Get what, Becky?" He began to fight back.

"I guess you don't get how poor I am!"

Silence filled the awkward space between them. In the distance, an errant bird cried out. Becky forced her breaths through her nose. Willing herself to breathe.

Zack stood and shoved his hands in his pockets. "I may not understand, Becky. But I love you. I'll always love you."

With that, he turned on his heel, skipped down the porch steps and trudged off to his truck. Becky watched him the whole way, her eyes burning.

As he pulled off in his truck, the tears came. Tears of shame. Tears of heartache. Tears every teenaged girl had cried before. But Becky seemed to cry them even harder.

Because Zack wasn't just a high school boyfriend. He was her soulmate.

But he didn't choose her.

At least, that's what Becky would tell herself for the next eighteen years.

Chapter 26

She took the afternoon to clear out her thoughts. Make a plan.

With Memaw darning socks in front of the television set, Becky holed up in her own room. She needed space to think. Really think, this time.

Her first step was to re-open her job search. For *real* this time. Becky hadn't found the New Albany postings in *The Hickory Grove Post*. Those, she'd found online.

But local Hickory Grove jobs didn't turn up online as easily. Her hometown was a bit behind the times, still. Now, she turned two pages in to find the classifieds, again taking up half a page. She creased the delicate paper and glanced around the differently sized boxes, looking for anything she'd missed earlier.

And then she saw it, splashed across the far page, sticking out like a tacky DUI criminal defense attorney's ad: Hickory Grove Realty. A secretarial position.

Perfect.

***

A half-hour later, she was standing in the muggy hallway of a converted office space. What used to be a cramped hallway now acted like a reception area. A *receptionist-less* reception area.

Finally, a gentleman appeared from a back room. Sweat crowned his bald head, and her face lit up when she saw him.

Old Mr. Hart, a jolly sort of man whose pudgy face strained across real estate signs as they poked their ways out of front lawns across town. His was the only recognizable realtor face in Hickory Grove. Partly because he'd always harbored a crush on Becky's mom.

"Rebecca Marie!" He boomed at her as he made his way over, nearly panting by the time they shook hands. "How is your mama!"

Becky's cheeks reddened slightly, but she smiled at his predictability. "She's, ah, she's doing well, Mr. Hart. In California these days."

His smile wavered only for a moment. "Call me Alan, Rebecca." He passed his hand out over the two broad-seated chairs that sat at crooked angles toward each other in front of a coffee table.

"Well, Alan. I'm here about your job posting," Becky announced with every bit of confidence she could muster. A local job was perfect. It was always the best choice. She could stay in town. Avoiding Zack would be a challenge, but Becky's priority to keep Memaw at the farm pushed to the forefront of her mind as soon as she called and cancelled her interview for that morning.

And, anyway, she loved watching HGTV and reading *Better Homes and Gardens*. Her favorite segments included the latest trends on how to arrange one's bookshelf. Fascinating stuff.

Maybe Becky wasn't born to work with books. Maybe she was born to work with the houses where books could live.

"So you're back in town for good, I take it?" He pried, dabbing his forehead with a handkerchief. And image of Grandbern flashed through Becky's mind, and she thought she might start bawling then and there.

She swallowed hard and nodded her head. "That's right, sir. Hoping to help my grandmother. You know how it is."

Her pause gave him a chance to allow a frown to settle across his mustachioed mouth. "I'm so terribly sorry to hear about Bernie, Rebecca. I attended the service. It was lovely. I hope you all are doin' okay down there off Main." He dipped his head and raised his eyebrows toward her.

Warmth spread through Becky's body, and she knew she was making the right choice. Home. Hickory Grove *was still home*.

Chapter 27

Two weeks had passed.

Time in which Becky quickly discovered just how much work it would be to act as Alan Hart's right-hand woman. Not only was his the only real estate office in town. He also acted as a broker and real estate tax attorney. His work with the local mortgage lender was nearly a full-time job in and of itself.

Alan Hart didn't merely need a secretary. He needed an entire staff. Up until this, he'd been outsourcing administrative work to his wife and daughter. But, apparently, they were drowning.

Becky didn't know the business, but she stepped in as well as she could, learning quickly and working twelve hour days to get a handle on the one transaction she'd been assigned.

On day fourteen, at exactly 4:45 P.M., Becky made the decision to call it quits by five. She wanted to take her two days to head north and visit Theo. She missed him terribly. And she needed a distraction. She'd been avoiding going anywhere public at normal hours in an effort to keep away from Zack and ignore any progress on the schoolhouse.

So far, nothing had happened. It was just a matter of days, though. She knew that much.

"Alan, I'm going to wrap it up and head home, if that's all right by you?" she called down the hall toward his office.

He answered her through a yawn as he trudged up the hall. "Sure is, Becky. That's just fine by me. You deserve a little rest, darlin'. You work too hard." He gave her a fatherly smile and held out a stack of papers. "Before you go, Becky Marie—" he began.

Becky didn't mind Mr. Hart's nicknames for her. She loved them, in fact. They made her feel at home. He was a gentle, kind man.

"Yessir?" she asked, her accent had begun to return to her, especially under the supervision of a truly southern man such as Mr. Alan Hart.

"Will you drop these two closing packets in the mail on your way home?"

"Sure thing, Alan." Becky reached for the thick packet and grabbed two manila envelopes from her carefully organized desk. One for the seller. One for the buyer.

She grabbed a pen then sat to find the addressee and transfer their mailing information onto the form envelope. Mr. Hart preferred pen and paper transactions. Emailing was beyond him. It didn't much matter in Hickory Grove. Everyone else pretty much did the same. Still, Becky insisted on following up with email correspondence. She'd get him to convert yet, she'd said.

This week, Becky had only assisted on one personal real estate transaction. It was a family home up by the school. She was responsible for filling out the closing paperwork and handling the escrow.

Becky knew Mr. Hart was juggling about ten other transactions at that time, but she was not yet familiar with the sellers or buyers.

But, she was a fast learner, and she could figure out how to address an envelope and send closing paperwork. Easy peasy.

Her eyes slid down the front page, skipping through tiny type-written contact information until her eyes found the mailing address line.

1200 East Douglas Avenue.

It was entirely familiar. Becky *knew* that address. She just couldn't put a finger on it.

Quickly, she glanced back up above the address line, searching for the name of the seller.

Hickory Grove Unified School District.

She raised her eyebrows, surprised to see a real estate transaction for the school district. Such a thing surely would have made the news.

Then again, Becky did not read or watch the news. Hadn't in two weeks. Ever since she scored this job.

She glanced at the clock to see it was closing in on five, but her curiosity pulled her deeper into her seat.

She studied the paperwork harder, searching for the property in question. The property the school was selling.

And there, plain as day, she saw it.

92 South Overlook Lane

Hickory Grove, Indiana

The schoolhouse.

Becky's chest burned. Tears stung her eyes.

Confused and panicked, she shuffled through the pages, the information blurring in front of her as her breath grew shallow. She considered calling out to Mr. Hart for help. For an explanation. Something. Anything.

But her voice was caught in her throat. She pressed the pages down onto the desk then pulled her hands to her head and rubbed at her temples.

The noise of tires crunched across the gravel just outside the real estate office. Becky couldn't look up. She couldn't deal with a customer. Not right now.

She had to get to the bottom of this. Had to know. *Who? Why? How?*

Becky swallowed and trained her eyes on the packet once again, this time squinting through her own tears for the word *Buyer*. A car door opened and slammed shut outside. Footsteps plodded up the front porch.

She forced herself to breathe, reading as fast as her eyes would go.

And then, just as the footsteps echoed from the other side of the front door, she found it.

Buyer's Name.

Becky sucked in a breath. At the same moment she saw the name, the front door swung open.

Zachary Michael Durbin.

Her eyes flashed up, and her heart raced in her chest. *"Zack?"*

Chapter 28

"Hi," he said, nearing her desk slowly. His eyes trained on her. His expression full of mischief.

But Becky was confused. "What are you doing here?" she asked, glancing behind her and down the hall toward Mr. Hart's office.

"To pick up my paperwork," he replied. "I just got off the phone with Alan. He told me you were about to mail it, but I was close by. I figured I'd just stop in. Get it myself." A smile danced across his lips.

Becky rose from her chair and cornered the desk, joining him in front of it. They stood a foot apart. Her eyes peering up. She licked her lips. "You—you're buying the *schoolhouse*?"

He nodded slowly, carefully, as though he didn't want to startle her. "Yes," he whispered.

"But how? Why?" It wasn't adding up.

"How? Well, I got an advance on my father's inheritance. I had to beg and plead, but once I showed him Mom's book—the one I found there—he gave in."

"Okay," Becky replied, her mouth hanging open as she blinked a few times. "And . . . what are you going to do with it?"

He laughed. A light, happy laugh. "Becky. I'll do whatever you need me to do. I'm decent with a hammer. I can throw up some drywall. It's up to you, girl," he drawled.

Becky felt her knees grow weak. "Are you saying—" she sputtered, bracing herself against the desk behind her.

Zack reached a hand out and gripped her waist, pulling her forward. "I'm saying I bought the schoolhouse. And I'm ready to help you with it. I'll be your investor. You can open a shop or a school or a library or whatever you want. We'll figure out the details later. An agreement of some kind. But, Becky," he paused long enough for her to bring her hands to his chest and lean into him. "It's yours, girl. I bought it *for you*."

When the words fell out of his mouth, she fell into him, her hand lacing up behind his neck. He replied in kind, pulling her into him and holding her there, against his body as she wept quietly into his neck.

He buried his face in the top of her head, kissing her and running his fingers up through her hair.

"I hope this doesn't mean you're gonna quit, Becky Marie." Mr. Hart's warm voice interrupted them, and Becky dropped back down onto her heels, wiping at her eyes with the back of her hand.

She let out a laugh and smiled at the old man. "Alan Hart, were *you* in on this?"

Zack laughed too, and Mr. Hart held up his palms. "Don't shoot the messenger!" he pleaded playfully.

Becky looked between the two men, amazed at the ruse. And grateful. More than anything, grateful.

Zack asked Mr. Hart if he could steal Becky for the rest of the evening, and he gave him the go ahead, reminding Zack that Becky didn't need anyone's permission. She was free to do as she saw fit.

Once they were in his truck, making a beeline for the schoolhouse, Becky thought about her boss's words. She felt free. Finally.

As Zack pulled his truck down the road and parked at the end of the dusty old path that led to her place—*their* place—a worry swelled in her.

"Zack, you didn't have to do this."

"Becky," he began, reaching for her hand and lacing his fingers through hers. "I know that. And I also know that if you could have bought this place—or leased it, or whatever—you would have. And, you know what? I would have done it a lot sooner had I not been so afraid."

"Afraid of what?" she asked, throwing him a sidelong glance.

"Afraid of a lot things. Undermining my own authority at work. Asking my dad for help. Taking a risk."

Silently, she nodded. "I'm sorry for what I said," she replied at last, squeezing his hand.

"Don't be," Zack answered. "It was the boost I needed. I've spent the last eighteen years waiting for my life to happen. Waiting on you. Or someone else, for that matter. Waiting on a promotion or a different opportunity. Then you showed back up. Beautiful as ever. Sweet as pie. Same girl I fell in love with all those years ago. And you didn't change one bit. I guess I didn't either. But, Becky. *Something* had to give, right?"

He stared ahead out the windshield and into the woods where children of yesteryear would go to gather tinder for their little stove.

"I guess so," she answered, slipping her hand from his and unbuckling her seatbelt.

"What are you doing?" he asked as she opened the door and jumped down onto the road.

"Zack Durbin, I hope you realize what kind of commitment this is," she said and slammed the door shut before running around the truck and to his side, where she stopped on the path, her arms spread out as she spun in a circle.

He popped out of his side and joined her. "What are you talking about?" he asked as he laughed and stepped forward, swooping in toward her and scooping her up into his arms.

"I mean, you just bought me my dream house," she answered, tossing back her head and giggling wildly.

"Well, as long as you come home to me at night, I think I can handle that."

Becky lifted her head and pulled herself closer to his face. "Are you asking me to move in Zack?"

"You're the one who said I just made a big commitment, right?"

She smiled and shook her head. "I'll be your girlfriend, but I'm not moving in with you yet, even *if* you just bought me a house."

"I'll take girlfriend. *For now*," he whispered into her ear.

Becky dropped her face to his and held his head in her hands, pulling him closer. "Zack," she whispered in response. "I love you."

"I love you, too, Becky. I always have. I always will."

She pressed her mouth onto his and their lips parted in tandem. It felt like their first kiss all over again. A single tear made its way down Becky's cheek, dropping from her jaw onto Zack's hand.

"Becky," he murmured as they each took a breath. "Now you're really stuck in Hickory Grove."

"Zack," she murmured back, interrupting herself to dip in for another kiss before running her own tongue over her lips and going on. "You didn't have to buy this place to keep me here. I would have stayed anyway. It might have taken me a while, but I came back for you, and I was going to stay for *you*."

And in that moment, Becky realized it was true. She didn't come back to Hickory Grove for the schoolhouse. Or even for Maggie or Grandbern or Memaw.

She came back for her heart.

Five Years Later

"Here, we go, Theo! Coffee and sustenance for the long day ahead. It's about to get crazy. Are you ready?" Becky cheered as she stomped her feet off at the back door and breezed in with a brown paper bag and a tray of three to-go coffees.

"Ready as I'll ever be," he answered, shuffling bills inside the till then sliding it shut and rising from his seat. "Here, let me help you." Theo reached for her goodies and set them on the side table behind The Teacher's Desk. She watched him for a moment, feeling herself glow with pride at her son. He would be starting his second year of the Eller School of Law in Tucson. Much like Becky, Theo wanted to return home. She couldn't begrudge him that.

Nor would she want to. After all, her fresh start had taken the exact shape she wanted it to.

Theo took a bite of his donut, fresh from Mally's—*Bill's* Mally's. Becky had grown to like the new menu just fine. It would never be the original. But sometimes, that was okay.

"Mom, did you see that line?" Theo asked between mouthfuls.

Becky nodded. "What did I tell you? This is exactly why I've been nagging Zack about an annex. Each year it's gotten worse. Mark my words: half of those people are from out of town."

Theo smiled and nodded then sipped his coffee as he stowed the book he'd brought along for his break.

"Any sign of Maggie, yet?" Becky asked as she bustled about, shifting her product displays just so and smoothing the lace curtains into place before striding to the front door.

Maggie had been responsible for quite a bit of the renovation, in fact. Her sense of style came in handy when Becky decided to mix farmhouse chic with a classic bookshop look.

Theo answered, "Yep. She's out front with Briar. They wanted to 'participate' this year. Whatever that means."

Becky smiled at the thought of Maggie's little girl. Briar was about to start second grade. No more little kid stuff. No more playing with dolls behind the cash register. She wanted to *participate*.

With a deep, satisfying breath, Becky twisted the antique lock from inside and pressed the door open as the old iron bell above clanged cheerfully.

Outside the front stoop a sizable crowd of parents and children alike were waiting for her. The kids milled around along the side yard which Zack had converted into a quaint play area, complete with two tire swings and a wooden see-saw.

Parents stood in casual huddles in front of her flowers and trailed along the new cobble-stone path almost all the way to the road.

They were all here for her annual back-to-school book fair.

"Welcome, welcome!" she chirped to the crowd. "Before you come in, a few quick tips to navigate today."

The bright-eyed group hushed in anticipation.

"We're a small store, but we're packed to the brim. You'll find our bookshelves and display cases are organized according to the Dewey Decimal System, and if you don't know what that is, come see me at the help desk in the back. There, you can munch on a cookie while I give you a brief overview. If it's too crowded inside, you and your children are welcome to take the little walking tour we've set up around the property." Becky pointed toward an official Indiana State Historical Society display stand that sprouted from the western corner of the shop. "This sign here will give you an overview of the history, and I also have pamphlets inside with more information. You'll get one with your goodie bag before leaving today." Becky caught sight of Maggie and Briar and winked at them. Briar waved back, and Maggie nodded Becky on. So, she clapped her hands together. "That's about it!" Then, with a professional affect, she stepped aside and waved her hand toward the open door.

In five years' time, Becky had become a woman who had everything she ever wanted—Theo home for summer break; a home with the man who resurrected his father's law firm, the man who resurrected her heart; and the promise of another warm batch of cookies from Memaw. Happiness didn't come any sweeter. And though Becky had help along the way, there was a tug inside her. A reminder that she was *Rebecca Durbin*. A woman who fought for what she wanted.

And a woman who got it.

She smiled broadly at her customers. Hickory Grove school children. Louisville and New Albany tourists. People, young and old, who loved books. Finally, Becky announced, "Welcome to *The Schoolhouse!*"

***

Thank you for reading *The Schoolhouse*. Learn more about the author and this series by joining her book club at elizabethbromke.com.

Acknowledgements

With each novel I write, I pull from a greater support network than the one before. I'd like to thank Judy Peterson for her expertise in the craft of narrative fiction. Also, Rachael Bloome, Kaci Lane Hindman, and Carina Taylor—romance writers who know so intimately how to improve upon a budding love connection. Thank you. Krissy Moran, my proofreader—thank you for your careful notes and support. Jessica Parker, thank you for your hard work on pulling together the *perfect* cover.

A big hug to my grandparents, who were models for the kind and loving characters within: Memaw, Grandbob, Grandma E., and Grandpa E. (in Heaven). Thank you.

Mom and Dad, thank you.

Always, I write for my family. I love you Ed and Little E.

CPSIA information can be obtained
at www.ICGtesting.com
Printed in the USA
LVHW090402130320
649838LV00004B/138